Risk Free Technology

Risk Free Technology

How small to medium businesses can stem huge losses from poorly performing IT systems

Charles L. Nault

GLOBAL
professional
publishing

Global Professional Publishing
Random Acres
Slip Mill Lane
Hawkhurst
Cranbrook
Kent TN18 5AD

Email: publishing@gppbooks.com

ISBN 978-1-906403-09-6

Printed in the United States by IBT

Contents

Introduction

Every two minutes two million e-mails are sent, 1,157 YouTube videos are viewed, 11,000 songs are downloaded, and 2 new blog sites are created. Those are just a few of the activities going on via the Internet. E-mail has evolved to become a mission-critical application as essential as electricity or telephone service. In fact, according to a META Group survey, 80 percent of corporate e-mail users believe that e-mail is far more valuable than telephone for business communications. Today, 90 percent of corporate communication is driven by e-mail.

In the 20+ years that I have been working on the implementation of technology into other people's businesses I have seen just about every level of implementation and network design and configuration that you can imagine. I've worked on networks for major carriers, foreign government, Fortune 500 companies, and 10 person firms.

Organizations from multi-billion dollar corporations to the community church have in common that they rely entirely on their e-mail, web access, and computer applications every moment of the working day. Any company that is going to compete and thrive in this world is going to do so through the effective use of technology. The optimal word is *effective*.

When they cannot effectively use the computer, I've observed, most employees chat with other employees and accomplish little or nothing. As a small business owner, when I see idle people in a business I can't help but think about the cost of all that idleness. In the ultra-competitive business world, the ability to leverage every hour of every worker's time for maximum productivity is essential to the very survival of an organization. Business managers and owners go to great lengths to leverage employees' time. There are startling statistics that show that the technology in most of these companies doesn't work a frightening percentage of the time.

Just how effective is IT in business? The only word that comes to mind is dismal. The facts speak for themselves. 78 percent of companies rate their IT as ineffective. Over 25 percent of IT projects are completed late. Studies from KPMG estimate that less than 40 percent of implemented projects, when measured one year later, showed any of their estimated business, value whether delivered on time or not. Businesses view e-mail as a mission-critical application but they're putting up with, on average, 1.6 downtime periods a month. 75 percent of businesses experienced an e-mail outage in 2005 with 72 percent of outages lasting for four hours or more. Poor system performance is number one on the top-five list of technology problems small businesses face according to July 2007 information from support.com. IT is just not effective. And downtime, as we'll see in much greater detail, is a constant issue.

Most people approach downtime from the viewpoint that you must protect your network from malicious attacks. There are real threats and we will spend significant time on the need to protect your network properly to avoid malicious downtime in this book. Small to medium businesses lose a half percent of their revenues to security attacks.

However, there is an even more significant problem with your network that has to do with daily performance. Total IT downtime costs companies an average of 3.6 percent of gross revenues according to Infonetics, one of the most respected IT research firms. Statistics show that this year you will bleed money while your workers sit idle because your network is not functioning correctly, or is not functioning at all. It will have nothing to do with any outside force attacking you. I can guarantee that it will happen to you. Non-malicious downtime is going to cost you money this year. The question is simply how frequent and how bad will your network outages will be?

A recent speaker at the CEO Club that I belong to said, "I'm not telling you anything you don't already know, or haven't heard before...the problem is execution." He was talking about leadership. And we as the audience collectively nodded our heads. This was a room full of CEOs. We all know that the problem of sub-maximum performance is often in the execution. It is even more so in the arena of Information Technology (IT). There are a lot of ways to execute in IT. There are right ways and wrong ways. Statistics assert that small to medium businesses do it wrong more than right.

So how do you get it right? Much of the current banter in the IT industry focuses on the concept of alignment. Alignment is touted as the silver bullet for getting IT costs under control and for getting the most from your IT investments. I will talk about alignment and how you can work towards alignment in your own company because it is important. You have to focus first on making IT effective. The objective of this book is to help you make your IT more effective. If you try to do alignment on a network that is ineffective, you will waste a lot of money and get extremely frustrated. 85 percent of business executives characterized their IT operations as ineffective when viewed from the perspective of how well their IT performed when aligned with their business objectives.

I am not suggesting alignment is a bad thing. I am telling you it is only a good thing if you first implement the suggestions in this book in order to make your Information Technology more effective. In part of the same study, companies achieving

2

effectiveness and alignment saw their three-year compound annual growth rate jump 37 percent, while IT spending rates dropped by more than 10 percent. Companies that achieved effectiveness but not alignment still cut IT spending by more than 17 percent and boosted growth by more than 10 percent. You simply cannot do alignment on an ineffective IT network and the statistics show that most IT networks are not effective.

How do the experts deal with these facts? They say alignment is not enough. Alignment needs to mature to the point where you don't just align your IT to your business objectives, you synchronize your objectives with your IT strategy. Again, a great idea. To take it even further the experts say, you get to the point where you design your own products and services, marketing plans, and delivery mechanisms in concert with your strategy for delivering IT services. This has been called convergence (though this term is also used in IT to describe the combining of voice/data/etc onto one ubiquitous network) and I've also seen it called Breakthrough IT. This is all wonderful if the network delivering all this great strategic stuff is rock solid and effective. If it is not, you will still be bleeding money.

What do IT leaders plan to do about this? Exactly the opposite of what they should be doing. A survey of IT leaders indicates that their number one priority in 2008 was to squeeze their vendors for lower prices. I almost fell on the floor when I read that. This was a survey of hundreds of top IT leaders. The total cost of ownership of any networking solution is primarily made up of the deployment and integration, regular upgrade, maintenance and support, and administration and management of that solution. The procurement cost of the equipment is widely recognized as a small fraction of the cost. The focus needs to be on reducing the on-going cost of the solutions. Most of that support is performed by IT staff in small to medium businesses. These folks are severely overworked and perform most of their tasks manually or with a hodgepodge of band-aid solutions that they have been forced to put in place because the owners/senior managers of their companies do not give them the funding they need to do things right, and do not take a vested interest in their success.

The only answer is a complete mind-set change of your view of IT. Senior managers and business owners of small- to medium-sized companies see IT as a necessary evil. It is no wonder, with the results we've just looked at. The answers that senior managers typically come up with are cost cutting measures. IT is just too expensive. What we have to do is find ways to cut costs. The pressure on IT to cut costs has been extraordinary in the past few years. Some of that is due to the fact that a lot of IT folks spent a lot of money and had very low returns on those investments in the early 90s. That's where the alignment concept came from when the economy slowed in the late 90s and early 2000; trying to ensure that IT only spends money on technologies that drive revenues or cut costs. The problem is that while the economy tightened up, the pace of technology accelerated at the highest rate in history. Even after the dot.com bubble burst, use of the Internet continued to explode – and so did dependency upon the services it provides, such as e-mail and e-commerce, remote access, and personal communications devices.

You have no choice but to view IT as a vital strategic service within your business. From this vantage point you need to be prepared to invest more in IT, at least in the short term. You only have the right to demand better performance from IT investment if you are willing to take a vested interest in your IT network, and in making sure it is performing at maximum effectiveness. In all likelihood you are clueless at how to approach this, or where to start. You're going to need help...

Most business owners have formed strong relationships with trusted outside advisors regarding the critical areas of banking, accounting, insurance, and legal issues. In fact, that same CEO Club that I belong to advocates that the most important relationships for a business owner are those relationships. While they are critical to your business, I would argue that a *more* critical relationship is one with a competent IT partner.

There is no one single factor that has more to do with the every-day performance of your businesses than the condition of your IT network. You, as the business owner or senior executive, are expected to know your company's revenues, debt, production levels, etc. right off the top of your head. You should be just as knowledgeable as to how effective your IT network is. You cannot do that alone. And you can't have your son, or nephew, or cousin's sister-in-law do it alone either – just as in all likelihood you cannot write your own contracts or audit your own books or self-insure your business, or would trust a relative who "dabbles in this stuff" to do it. Surveys say that is what you are trying to do. Even if you have the rare company that enjoys high margins and low overhead, giving you an enormous budget to get this done, you won't be able to find, and keep, the staff to do it all. Right now, there is a major shortage of technical talent. In fact as of January of 2008 IT unemployment is statistically at "0". That trend is going to continue.

You need to engage a qualified IT partner and assure that partner becomes your trusted advisor on Information Technology. Your own IT staff, regardless of the size of that staff, has to merge with the staff of that trusted partner in order to assure maximum effectiveness in all of the critical aspects of your network. A 2006 study by *VAR Business* magazine found that nearly half of the small to medium sized businesses who installed networking solutions on their own ended up calling a network integrator to correct mistakes done during installation. Have you ever seen this sign hanging in an automotive service center: "Hourly labor rate $45.00, $55.00 if you watch, $65.00 if you help!"?

We will discuss how to build or to adjust your own staff to assure that they will effectively engage your IT partner. We'll also provide conceptual details for each of the major layers for building an effective IT network. This will not be an in-depth technical discussion. Instead at each layer we will look at some of the critical decisions that must be made to ensure IT effectiveness. We cannot cover all of them in one book, nor do we intend to even come close. What we will do is look at enough of them for you to become engaged in meaningful dialogue with your staff. Being engaged in IT means that you take the time to understand, from a business not a technical perspective, what is critical at each layer, and make an informed decision as to how to invest wisely in success at that layer. This takes time which you have precious little of. Rather than reading the entire book from cover to cover – which most senior executives rarely do anyway – we'll give you the opportunity to quickly assess your current effectiveness so that if there are areas where your company already does extremely well, you won't waste time reviewing that topic in detail.

Change is extremely difficult. According to the book *Change or Die* by Alan Deutschman, 90 percent of heart patients who were given the choice to either change to a healthier lifestyle or face imminent death did not change. Deutschman points out that lasting change requires a completely new way of viewing the problem, and the hope that real change is possible. We don't change based on fear alone. As you read in the first chapter of *Risk Free Technology*, the facts will scare you. That fear will not likely be enough for you to adopt a completely new mindset.

Deutschman's research indicates that lasting change requires an agent of change; someone who believes wholeheartedly in the *ability* to change and leads the charge. In your company, you need to lead the charge. How do I know this? I have been dealing with IT folks my entire career, and many of them are dying for the people at the top of their companies to take a more strategic view of IT and to give IT the necessary focus to really bring about change. In short; real, effective, lasting change will not occur without your direct attention.

You must gain a *new perspective* on the importance of your network. The buck must stop with *you* for how well it performs. You must have your *finger on the pulse* and know ahead of time if a problem is creeping up, so you can assure it is dealt with before it costs you money, reputation, etc. If you really do make the effort to change, your business will benefit tremendously. Look again at the statistics: Companies achieving effectiveness *and* alignment saw their three-year compound annual growth rate jump 37 percent, while IT spending rates dropped by more than 10 percent. Companies that achieved effectiveness but not alignment still cut IT spending by more than 17 percent and boosted growth by more than 10 percent. I am certain the drops in IT spending were not squeezed out of their vendors. They were the result of wisely investing in the right solutions to reduce the total cost of ownership, as evidenced by their impressive growth rates.

By following the advice we present here, and thus making your IT more effective, you can *stop the bleeding…*

Chapter 1
The Problem

According to an article published in May 2007 by Paul Weinberg, only 22 percent of over 100 companies surveyed indicated that their Information Technology (IT) department functioned effectively. That is an incredible statistic! Suppose one out of five medical operations were successful. What if over 70 percent of the contracts your lawyer drew up for you were flawed? Or maybe your financial reports were only accurate say, 25 percent of the time. Would you not be outraged? "Well yes, but IT is a complicated business and the measure of effectiveness is subjective when it comes to my network and computer applications," you might argue. Hogwash I say, and research supports me on this.

The IT industry measures effectiveness in terms of uptime – the times when your users (be they employees or clients) have no problem getting to, and using, the critical applications that make the smooth operation of your business possible. The opposite of uptime is of course, downtime – the times when your users beat their keyboards, smack their screens, or slam down the phone in frustration and disgust. It is in those moments that everything about you and your business comes into question. The employee is asking questions like "How do they expect me to do my job when I can't get to the Web, or send an e-mail" or "What kind of two bit operation am I working for?" The client is asking "Why are we doing business with such a messed up operation?" or worse, "Who else can we get to fill this need?" As a business owner, I cringe at the very idea that any of these questions are being asked about my business at any moment of the day. There are times when it has kept me up at night. I worry about the effect on morale internally, and the possible loss of business externally. As bad as that is, it is only in the last few years that I have added to my worries because I've gained a clear understanding that the cost of downtime is measured not just in terms of reputation and lost business, but in terms of actual dollars of lost productivity…and those costs are astounding.

The average company experiences 501 hours of network downtime every year, according to a study conducted by Infonetics Research. "Overall downtime costs an average 3.6% of annual revenue…" says Jeff Wilson, principal analyst of Infonetics Research (www.infonetics.com) and author of the study, titled *The Costs of Enterprise Downtime*, North America 2004.

Let that sink in for a moment, especially if you're a business owner, or a senior manager responsible for profitability. You are bleeding money in lost productivity due to poor network performance. I know from personal experience that some companies in the survey don't need this book to tell them how serious this is. In fact, they have implemented the necessary systems to assure that they beat the odds. They have very little downtime but, keep in mind, they are included in the statistics. Chances are that if you are reading this book to get a better grip on your company's technology, your numbers are even worse. So let me ask you; How hard have you worked this past year to increase your company's revenues? I know how hard our management team has worked. To compensate for this downtime, if my company were to experience the industry average 501 hours, we would need to add over $1M in additional sales. To do so, we would have a few options. We could add a seasoned sales person to the team, carve out a portion of our territory for him/her to cultivate, provide a reasonable base salary, and probably a decent draw against future sales during an agreed ramp up period. Chances are this person would still take at least a year to ramp up.

We could design and implement a new service product for our existing customer base. Historically, the most effective new service product we ever introduced produced around $1M in gross revenue the first year. Most others took closer to three years to achieve that level of sales. We would need to come up with the idea, mold it into a saleable service, establish a pricing structure, implement all of the back-end processes and procedures for delivery, accounting, and lifecycle management of the service, come up with a marketing plan, train our sales force, and roll it out to our existing customer base.

We could get real fortunate and discover a new product from either an existing or new vendor, that we think will not only be a tremendous benefit to our customers but would provide an additive revenue stream of $1M dollars in the first year we carry it. We still have to go through all of the back-end work, training, etc. Again, experience has proven that it is highly unlikely that the first year would produce anywhere near those results. Every one of these potential revenue enhancing strategies is expensive and carries no guarantee of success.

Instead what we could do is to take some pro-active steps to ensure that we experience far less downtime than that scary industry average. The Infonetics research reveals the numbers in a very real, practical sense. That gives us the ability to do some very basic calculations regarding the costs of downtime. If you look at the revenue your company produces, and evaluate that in terms of revenue per employee, you can gain some key insight as to what it costs your business to have those people sitting idle. We have developed a spreadsheet that does exactly that for you. This is strictly a strategic, bottom line business tool. It looks at your business the way a board member likely would. When you have a discussion at the Board level about getting maximum productivity (leverage) from every hire, you might view it in terms of how much each employee generates in revenue on average, and how much that employee contributes to the bottom line Earnings Before Interest, Taxes, Depreciation, and Amortization (EBITDA). I can tell you that in technology companies those two numbers are what it really boils down to. Revenue Per Employee tells us how well we are leveraging our resources, and EBITDA tells us what we are really worth as a company in terms of earnings and earning potential. So that is the perspective with which this tool was developed (see Figure 1.1). For this example I have plugged in some basic numbers for a fictitious 100 person company. The weighted (including all benefits) average hourly cost per employee is around $24.00. Each employee generates a little over $100.00 in revenue per hour. Based on this company's bottom line the profit (EBITDA) per employee is $4.55 per hour. The tool we use includes a pull down that allows you to select an uptime percentage. In this case I have chosen 95 percent uptime. This is slightly better than the industry average, and results in about 437 hours of downtime. I have been extremely conservative to indicate that the average outage is one hour long and affects 30 percent of the employees in the company. In reality that company will have outages of varying durations.

One company hired us to completely redesign their network from the ground up after sending literally thousands of employees home for eight hours while their network was crippled by an outage. As an FYI, five years later, we are upgrading the entire network. In the five year period there was never an outage that affected anywhere near 100 percent of their employees. In fact, according to their senior management all downtime was planned downtime during that period. It was they who made the decision that we should also do the upgrade.

Annual Cost of Downtime Worksheet

General Factors	
Enter last year's total revenues	$20,000,000.00
Enter last year's EBITDA	$837,527.00
Enter the total number of employees	100
Enter the average employee cost per hour	$ 24.00
Revenues per hour per employer	$ 108.70
EBITDA per hour per employee	$ 4.55
Days per week of business operations	5
Hours of operations	8
Number of holidays operations are closed	10
Number of annual business hours	2000

		Loss Revenue	Loss EBITA
Enter the number of hours for an outage	1	$ 10,869.57	$ 455.18
Enter the percent of the company affected	30%	$ 3,260.87	$ 136.55

		Loss Revenue	Loss EBITA
Enter the desired uptime level	95.000%		
Number of outage hours per year	437.10	$ 4,751,086.96	$ 198,958.18
Number of outage minutes per year	26226.00		

Figure 1.1

The number of employees affected by each outage for our fictitious company will vary as well. I made both entries conservative, so as not to stack the deck in favor of my premise here. The bottom line on this example is that our little company here bleeds almost $200,000.00 in bottom line profits every year – and they are doing slightly better than the average small- to medium-sized business in the US.

I realize that this is a pretty simple spreadsheet. I have found in the last 20 years, that the more simple and straightforward I can make the information I need regarding decisions about my business, the easier it is to convince others involved in the decision-making process, and the easier it is to measure the results. The more complex the information the less likely I am to get consensus and buy-in, and the harder the results are to measure.

It certainly doesn't take an economics degree to see that this is a lot of money to lose for no good reason just poor execution. It is worth saying again and again, that it doesn't take a lot more money to do things right. IT is expensive. It is expensive even if you do it wrong. Even if your attitude is that it is a necessary evil that you have to have, and that attitude is reflected in your budget, it still is expensive. A 100 person company will not need to spend $200,000.00 more a year to do it better.

Keep in mind that the previous discussion regarding all of the questions that pop up when a downtime incident occurs are not factored into these costs. It is not possible to quantify all of these issues.

Nagging questions do hit you hard in the event of any serious outage. Will you lose top quality employees who feel they really can't function to maximum potential? Will you lose that customer who got a ring-no-answer, or couldn't get to your website, or who was told by your own employee that "our systems are down right now, but they should be up soon..."? (How many times have you heard that?!) All very good questions and the likely answer is that you will lose employees and customers if your network fails too often. In fact *Contingency Management and Planning Magazine* says that 40 percent of companies surveyed viewed failure to meet customer expectations as the major cost of downtime besides productivity. Others thought the loss of their competitive advantage, and damage to their public image, was the greatest cost.

Where most small- to medium-sized businesses failed to adequately invest is at the core of their network, also known as the infrastructure. For the purpose of this book we will consider the network infrastructure to be all of the pieces that form the network that all of your computers, printers, and other peripheral devices (and possibly your phones) are connected to in order to communicate with each other, and with the outside world. We include all the connections internal to a building, and all the connections that get you out of the building to another internal company location, or to the Internet, or to a partner's network. I sometimes also refer to this as your backbone network. Like many of the basic terms in IT, the logic is clear once you know what it means. I found this to be true in the computer world. Data inside a computer for example rides on a connection called a bus. Computer processes are run on a Central Processing Unit (CPU), and instructions that stop that unit in order to make it do something different than what it is doing at the moment are referred to as interrupts.

While we do have a plethora of acronyms, many are a whole lot simpler than, say, medical terms like the ones that refer to bones in the body. Sensei Fred at the Jui Jitsu dojo where I attempted to learn self defense, liked to quiz us on the bones of the body. They just don't make any logical sense, except for perhaps the fact that meta is used for both the carpals and tarsal which are used to describe the fingers and toes. Our terms have typically been more basic. Once you connect that computer to any type of network, there is an accepted way for that computer to talk to other devices also on that network. Not surprisingly, the control of this communication is referred to as the protocol. Pretty simple. When I was in the Air Force, if I wanted to talk to the Base Commander, I had to follow protocol. When I hook up my computer, if it wants to talk to a higher-up device, it has to follow protocol. On the Internet, that communication protocol is called the Internet Protocol more commonly referred to as IP.

Some of the deeper terminology is just not worth knowing unless you are completely hands-on. Most of our terminology is quite descriptive of the actual function being performed, once you understand what the function is. So let's grab the most simple of medical terms, backbone, to describe the basic network to which everything else is connected. Thankfully we call remote locations branch offices and not tarsals. Keep in mind the synonymous terms of infrastructure and backbone and you'll be fine. I advocate that you stay away from many of the acronyms, and I'll explain why when we talk about educating your end users as part of your strategy. For now we need to get back to the network.

Your business needs are ever changing. Information technology changes faster than any other industry. These changes sometimes suggest, other times require, that you change your network. That great new software that you have decided will drive sales, or reduce inventory waste, or shorten your delivery cycle, will often require a network upgrade. When this is overlooked, and it often is, productivity is negatively affected across the board. It is a fact that most of the telephone systems being installed today are designed to operate on the very same network that carries your data. (Because the voice is converted into the same type of data that runs on the Internet – the Internet Protocol (IP) – it is referred to as IP Telephony (IPT)). That is good in many ways, bad in at least one – if your data network is down your company can't even make phone calls. The process of converting a voice conversation into a stream of data and then converting it back, along with the processes of setting up the calls and constantly reporting on the status of those calls, takes a lot of network resources. There are significant advantages to the new data-based phone systems. You can plug your desk phone into any jack at any location on your network and it will ring in and dial out as your extension. You can get your phone messages in your e-mail and vice-versa. This, along with a number of other great features, can provide a measurable increase in productivity. Much of the time though, the existing network needs a major upgrade to make the IP phone system perform effectively. Oftentimes this is overlooked when considering the cost of this new productivity tool. If you put an IPT system on an old network, not only does it function poorly, everything else you do on your network slows way down. Existing applications that used to run fine are reduced to a slow crawl with the demands of new applications on your backbone network.

One constant source of change has more to do with security than anything else. The hacker community, those dastardly folks who think creating havoc on computer networks is fun and challenging, spend much of their time trying to figure out ways to hijack the computers on your network. Forgive the simplicity here, but I have found that some business owners are not aware of the differences in the computers that run the applications such as e-mail, websites, etc. which are referred to as servers, and those that are used daily by employees. These could be desktop or laptop computers. A business owner told me just today that they don't run servers because they have a peer-to-peer network. He then went on to tell me that their company uses a Microsoft e-mail program called Exchange – which runs on a server. I'm not faulting the guy, it's easy to get confused, but in the same breath he told me that one of his managers had suggested that their company needed to consult with mine, and he disagreed because he "has this firmly under control", and his manager "just doesn't understand this stuff"...I just shook my head and walked away.

Anyway, the servers run on an entirely different operating system, referred to as server software. The most popular is made by Microsoft. There have been many iterations of server software from Microsoft, such as Windows NT, Windows 2000, Windows 2003 and most recently the new Vista software. (As an FYI, Exchange is an e-mail application that runs on a Microsoft server running one of these programs.) Being the most popular software in the world makes it also the biggest target for the hacker community. There is a never-ending cycle of hackers discovering vulnerabilities in the operating system. When you read about someone hacking into a company or branch of government computer, it is most likely to be the result of a vulnerability in the operating system running on their servers. Other systems are hardly immune to attack. A January 2008 attack hit over 10,000 Linux (an alternative to the Microsoft operating system) web servers, and infected any user who visited the websites on those servers, and whose computer did not have the latest fixes for known vulnerabilities in a number of very popular software applications.

Since I mentioned e-mail, I should also point out that a 2007 study titled *Planning for Improved E-mail Availability* conducted by Osterman Research for U.K.-based The Neverfail Group found that businesses are on average suffering 1.6 unscheduled e-mail outages a month. The amount of time the e-mail system is down varies considerably. Sometimes it's something simple that only knocks the e-mail system out for half an hour, but at other times, it's down for several hours. "E-mail is a critical tool as it's become an important line of internal and external communication," said Andrew Barnes, Senior Vice President of Corporate Development at The Neverfail Group. When e-mail goes down, it might only be a minor hassle, but it could also mean a negative impact on various elements of the business, including sales and customer service. No surprises there. One of the surprises of the survey was that although people recognize the importance of e-mail and the costs associated with e-mail outages, organizations are not proactively managing their e-mail systems. Often, IT does not even know the e-mail system is down until end-users start calling them with complaints – and it can take a variable amount of time before end-users notice they're not receiving e-mail.

One of the factors that make networking in many companies so much more difficult is the failure to standardize. I'll talk more on this point when we discuss the idea of a trusted partner. Please don't ignore this point: if you have a hodgepodge of different products purchased from the lowest bidders, with which your staff has pieced together a network, it stands to reason that the process of keeping track of this equipment and making sure all of it is up to date at all times becomes a much more complicated ordeal. It will cost you far more than you save.

When I talk later about security, I will discuss the policies you must enforce regarding who can do what. A precise, comprehensive, and strictly enforced security policy is critical. Unlike your other utilities, your network is a constant target for attack from the previously mentioned hacker community, who couldn't care less about your particular business. Taking networks down, or sending malicious information to others while making it appear to have come from you, and a variety of other foul, dastardly deeds are a game for them. They compete with each other in the design and deployment of these attacks. Many websites, blogs, forums, etc are dedicated to propagating this bane on our networking society. As bad as all that may sound, there are rock solid ways of staying ahead of these bandits. I have no desire to propagate the fear factors that many companies use to sell you (and sometimes over-sell you) a plethora of products to keep away the bad guys. Most of the downtime I have seen over the years is non-malicious. But I have seen malicious attacks. The worst of which was an attack that sent child pornography to the entire customer list of a small company. How much damage do you think that did to their reputation? How do you recover from that? It was a fairly easy problem to mitigate from a technical perspective, but the damage had already been done.

A lot of this really is procedural. No matter how good your systems are, your users determine how secure your network is day-to-day by the way they conduct themselves. The person who writes their Personal ID Number (PIN) on a sticker that they put on the back of their ATM card is likely to keep their password in close proximity to their computer, and in plain view. I have to wonder what people are thinking sometimes. In a 2007 survey conducted by DigitalPersona in conjunction with the Business Performance Management (BPM) Forum, almost 60 percent of respondents said that they had shared their network password with a colleague and 17 percent had either given out or received someone else's token or smart card. "As a result, people who are not entitled or not suppose to have access to certain applications might end up getting access to those applications," said Amr Assal, Senior Product Manager from DigitalPersona. "Once you start sharing passwords you really have no way of knowing what could happen," he added. The survey also found that 32 percent of respondents were looking for solutions that combine ease of use and increased productivity. 28 percent of respondents bought notebooks with fingerprint [authentication] embedded in them…62 percent said they hadn't used it! Please explain that to me if you are one of the people who paid for the fingerprint authentication…

Ageing equipment is also a factor. Technology has an effective lifecycle. What tends to happen is that companies wait until the equipment becomes obsolete, or is no longer supported by the manufacturer, or simply fails. There are countless times when I have seen an important project scrapped or postponed because of a reactive replacement of a failed piece of ageing equipment. The project was planned for a strategic business purpose that now has to wait for lack of sufficient funds.

Another less sinister, yet more costly source of downtime, is your own, well meaning employees. In fact, 22 percent of downtime is actually caused by accidents, referred to as operator error. It may be someone in your IT department who makes a simple mistake that takes down a critical server. It may be an employee who is somewhat tech savvy, who decides he/she needs something sooner than your IT staff can deliver it. I've seen networks slow to a crawl with a few rogue key strokes. I hate to admit this in print, but in some of my training sessions for various technology companies in the early years I sometimes used to refer to general users of technology as DAUs (translated Dumb A _ _ Users). I'm sure you can fill in the blanks. I also hate to admit that as technology has advanced there are times when I am a DAU myself. It's not always just general users who can be DAUs. One of the most embarrassing moments from the early days of my career was an incident in which I personally took down a company's entire network while installing a demonstration unit on a customer's site, in the middle of the work day. That was a long time ago, but the memory of it is seared into my mind. The networks we know today were still very new back then. Yet many employees were affected, and needless to say, I didn't get that particular deal. They were very polite and understanding as they walked me to the door. But they never returned my repeated phone calls after that.

I include my little war story just to point out that it is quite possible for one person to cripple your entire network if that network is not properly designed and implemented. Higher education is the most vulnerable organization for some fairly obvious reasons. Students from literally all over the world show up each semester fully expecting to connect their various laptops, audio and video devices, etc to the campus network. Most of these devices are a mess. (If you have a young teen at home you know what I'm talking about.) Cisco Systems had a cute commercial on TV for a while that showed a little girl taking down the network at her Dad's company by sitting at his desk and downloading some new games. It happens.

Jargon is the bane of IT's existence. Having worked for manufacturers I can tell you that a technology is barely in the conceptual phase before someone sticks an acronym on it. The day before I wrote this section I had a discussion with one of our own internal IT staff. In a ten minute time frame he managed to throw out at least a dozen acronyms that I was not familiar with – and I have spent my life in technology. You would think that he had been reviewing the complete expanse of our network, but he was just talking about one small part of our total technology implementation. In fact our discussion was limited to the storage of data and how the configuration of that storage affected our ability to run our critical servers in such as way that we would experience no downtime whatsoever should a single server crash. It is no wonder that most business owners and managers delegate most, if not all, of the decisions regarding technology to their IT department. By the way, this book is not going to remove the mystery of the technical acronyms. There are too many to even attempt to list them all here. We do provide a glossary of the terms used in this book. Beyond that though we would fill volumes to even start with the terms used in technology across a cross section of businesses. We would have to start with the terminology that describes some of the older solutions that may or may not apply to your network, depending on how current it is. Then we could move on to acronyms that apply to the most current technologies installed in most networks, and finally conclude with the new acronyms coming out to describe technologies still in the early adopter phase, some of which will catch on and become widely adapted, and others of which will fall by the wayside This is why I believe that unless you own or manage a firm specifically in the information technology field, it is a colossal waste of time to even try to learn all this stuff. Even the people who sell the technology realize what a problem their jargon is. Of course as with anything else, a problem spells opportunity. I recently read of a company that videotapes presentations by vendors in order to show them just how confusing all their jargon is to their intended audience, and then helps them to simplify the message. Imagine that! We techies are so far gone into the twilight zone we have to pay someone to get us back to earth! A recent survey by Ziff Davis published in their white paper *New Focus on IT Management* found that only 50 percent of respondents felt that the performance objectives of their Information Technology department were communicated effectively in understandable language. (Now you know why this book is not technical!)

The single greatest problem that exists in IT today is the lack of documentation of everything I have talked about, and will talk about, in this book. Complete, up-to-date documentation of exactly what is on the network, how it is configured, what revision of software it is running, etc. exists in very few organizations that I have seen over the years. It is a constantly moving target, usually administered by an understaffed, overworked group of people who are notoriously poor at organizing and recording information. This problem rears its ugly head at the very worst of times – when you are attempting to successfully add to or upgrade the network, and when the network is down. I have seen countless hours wasted when the people trying to do the implementation or fix the problem have been working with outdated information. It would be like trying to build a swingset with the wrong instructions. But not so blatantly wrong so that you could recognize that you've got a different model to these complex step-by-step instructions. More like a few bolt sizes being wrong in the directions so that when you get to the end you can't put the last few pieces on because those bolts are the wrong size. How long would it take you to retrace your steps and find those critical bolts? It could be hours and hours. If you're really sharp and experienced at putting swingsets together, you may recognize along the way that a particular bolt seems longer than it needs to be. You might then select the proper sized bolt, reserving the bolt you'll need later. That's a best case scenario. Now assume that you don't correct the directions and you can't finish the project. A helpful neighbor is going to finish it for you because you have a business trip to go on. You were tired and it was getting late, so you figured you'd just tell him about it the next day. You forgot. Now he continues where you left off not knowing there are a few more such instances. You're on the phone with him the next night and he laments at how he had to go back and exchange a number of bolts after it had taken him hours to find they were missing. Are you getting the idea? Sure swing sets are a pain to put together. They are nothing compared to networks.

I have to share this story with you. It is the moment when I got the idea for the first *Network as a Utility* article I wrote. I had to do something. You'll see why…

Just about a year ago I went to a multi-billion dollar company in New England that I wouldn't think of sharing the name of in print. I was dumbfounded by what I saw.

Here's how it all began: My company had hired a lead generation firm that focused entirely on C-Level meetings. They did a very good job of getting me in to see the CEO or CIO of companies around New England. I usually brought a sales person with me. I needed the salesperson there, to get beyond my usual spiel of who Atrion is, what our company was capable of, and our philosophy for doing business, and get down to a deeper understanding of the bits and bytes of the client's specific needs.

So, on this particular call, we arrived at our appointment and were told that the CIO of this multi-billion dollar company, doing business in 13 different countries, had decided that his main IT guy would be a better person for us to talk to. We waited in a makeshift employee cafeteria for quite some time until a young man with a sizeable belly and a buzz haircut, wearing jeans and a flannel shirt came over to ask if we were the guys from at-trion. (Our company name is pronounced A-tree-on.) He both apologized that we were meeting with him as opposed to the CIO, and indicated it would likely be a waste of time too since he had everything under control and didn't typically work with Value Added Resellers (VARs) like us. (We have worked extremely hard to move away from that title to that of a strategic partner – more on that in Chapter 5.)

Our host led us to a small makeshift room just about the size of a double walk in closet. It was about as cluttered an area as I had seen. Not atypical for a techie. He cleared books and papers off of a couple of chairs. We sat amazed for the next 20 minutes as he showed us all the free software and low cost network hardware, including home-made servers, that he had pieced together to form his company's network. He was quite proud that he was in the process of implementing IP telephones and an IP phone system running on a server he had built himself, as a reseller for a second tier PC manufacturer. To make sure that the network was always running, and that he had his finger on the pulse, he had installed free software called Big Brother. This network management software would page him any time the network experienced any type of hiccup. While he went through this presentation another young man entered. He was a junior-level technician just out of a Microsoft training class, who was our host's right-hand man though he seemed to have very little knowledge of the overall network and appeared merely task oriented. Our host was quite proud as he wrapped up his presentation and not so politely told us he really didn't need any help and was, again, sorry to have wasted our time. I left with my salesperson who was obviously disappointed – and with a very sick feeling in my stomach.

It had little to do with the fact that we had no opportunity there, or that I had just wasted an hour and a half drive, 30 minutes of waiting, and another 30 minutes on his presentation. It had everything to do with the fact that somebody owned this multi-billion dollar business, well over 1,000 people's livelihood depended on this business, and the entire core of the operation was entrusted to one cocky, out of shape young man, who, in the interests of job security, pieced together a hodgepodge network, did precious little documentation of what was there, and was the single point of failure and recovery for the entire company. At that moment I felt like I should do everything in my power to get to the CEO of that company and try to plead with him to do something to protect his company! Realizing that he would likely view me as an opportunist, and all I would do was to make the CIO and MIS manager hate my company and blacklist us forever I thought better of it. Instead I starting thinking about how to reach the thousands of folks just like him, who had no real clue, despite all the press, etc. around networks and security, about the time bomb that is their IT network. I decided right then to formulate the idea for this book.

Don't get me wrong, I am not suggesting that I have seen a lot of companies that size with anything that even slightly resembles this mess. I have seen a lot of networks that closely resembled this mess – they were just smaller companies! Enough of them in fact, that I just had to get on my soap box. That is what this book is, my soapbox. I am so adamantly convinced that this insanity has to be stopped that I am going to do everything in my power to convince you that not only do you owe it to your employees, customers, and suppliers, but that everything you have worked so hard for could be destroyed if you don't make sure that your computer/information network is as reliable as the power into your building.

We've been talking about the almost countless ways in which your network is, in all likelihood, bleeding money in terms of downtime. The remainder of this book is going to present the solutions to these problems in terms of how to design, implement, and maintain your network in a way that reduces downtime. Before we go there though, I would like to spend a little bit of time on the subject of general productivity. Productivity of course, is dramatically impacted by downtime. (I just read about software that measures and tracks employee productivity...I wonder what happens if the network goes down and you can't get to that application!!)

Productivity is also dramatically impacted by the absence of a strong, secure remote access solution. I can hardly believe that just a few days ago I read an article that said that an alarming number of small to medium business managers, 37 percent in fact, translate the idea of someone working from home into "I'm taking it easy today". There are a number of good reasons why employees should be enabled to work from home on a regular, planned basis, and – in the case of a snowstorm or sick child – on an emergency basis. In addition, with an effective remote access system your employees can extend the work day.

I started my business specifically so I could be home each night to read my kids a bedtime story and tuck them in. My previous positions required a lot of travel. Once the kids were in bed, I would always get back on the computer and get some customer quotes done in those early days. I didn't have remote access then, so I carried disks around. The applications were fairly limited, as were the resources I needed at the network. That would be impractical today. Most all of the applications we use today are centrally based, as, most likely, are yours. Your employees, given solid remote access, will be able to stop what they are doing in time to spend quality time with their families. Like me, once the kids are in bed, they can log back on and extend that work day. They are glad to have the opportunity to do so. It relieves pressure. If they don't take it to extremes, it enhances their family life (quality of life). Remote access is a tremendous boon to our productivity and it has been since the day we implemented it. The same study that said managers think working from home is slacking indicates that 68 percent of employees said they would be more productive and end up working longer hours. My experience in our company as well as with the companies with whom we've worked over the years is that a solid, dependable, always on, remote access system serves to not just dramatically improve productivity, but also to improve morale.

At a recent Rotary breakfast a fellow member who runs a small company that sells internationally, shared that he is extremely frustrated by their lack of technology and the impact on productivity. The owner of his company, who of course, was the founder and the brains behind the company's entire existence, enjoys technology. So he took it upon himself to put a network together, with the assistance of a young nephew. Sound familiar? He is an extremely bright and gifted chemical engineer who owns several significant patents. He is bright enough in fact to have taught himself technology. His network works, but as his general manager explained to me over breakfast, his international sales force still faxes orders in! The cost and the delays in doing so are nothing short of ridiculous. The General Manager however, is powerless to change the situation. How do you criticize the owner and founder without insulting him and his nephew? The answer is you don't. The GM has neither the time cycles, desire, or motivation, to attempt to change any of this. And in this particular case, it is not his place to do so. If you are such a business owner, put aside your ego and recognize it is your responsibility to get with the program and put technology to its full and proper potential. When you do, your network will make you money in increased productivity. The company in the example I sighted here could increase sales by 25-30 percent with a fully functional, secure remote access system for their sales force. Instead they will likely hire some extra sales folks, and hope they do well using the functioning but not ideal setup they have today. If the latter sounds like a viable solution to you, please reconsider before you continue to bleed money and damage morale.

I hope it is crystal clear to you that stopping the bleeding is the primary motivation for an entirely new way of looking at your network. Yes IT can be a real strategic advantage. Volumes have been, and continue to be, written about wonderful applications that provide real advantages. My experience is that the implementation and on-going performance of these great software applications in most small to mid-sized companies is severely hampered by your viewpoint that the infrastructure on which they run is nothing more than a nuisance. IT is a bottomless money pit, a source of constant headache, and is administered by difficult people who are hard to understand, let alone get along with. Until that viewpoint changes, you will not make real progress, even if you read this entire book. You'll be just like the 90 percent of heart attack victims one year from now.

Your network infrastructure is most likely broken. It is your fault and you have to fix it. You are responsible for making sure that your network infrastructure serves your company as reliably as any other utility and that:

1)   It does everything that your employees need to be as productive as they can be

2)   It works to full potential at all times

3)   It is kept current and secure

4)   It is thoroughly, accurately, consistently documented with up-to-date, detailed information.

If you get that, please read on. If not please stop right now and either send the book back to me or give it to another business owner/leader and challenge him/her to find value in it.

Chapter 2
The Solution

How reliable can your network be? To what extent can you effectively stop the bleeding? According to Cisco Systems, a leader in Information Technology solutions, the most reliable network is up 99.99947 percent of the time. American Power Conversion, a leading provider of power conditioning and back-up products considers 99.99962 percent to be the Holy Grail of uptime. In either case, this amounts to under six minutes of downtime per year. Figure 2.1 plugs in 99.999 percent uptime. This is what the IT industry refers to as achieving Five Nines. Compare that to the industry average of 501 hours, and the contrast is astounding! If we look at that number in terms of revenue loss it drops to almost nothing. The bleeding has stopped!.

General Factors	
Enter last year's total revenues	$20,000,000.00
Enter last year's EBITDA	$837,527.00
Enter the total number of employees	100
Enter the average employee cost per hour	$ 24.00
Revenues per hour per employer	$ 108.70
EBITDA per hour per employee	$ 4.55
Days per week of business operations	5
Hours of operations	8
Number of holidays operations are closed	10
Number of annual business hours	2000

General Factors			
		Loss Revenue	**Loss EBITA**
Enter the number of hours for an outage	1	$ 10,869.57	$ 455.18
Enter the percent of the company affected	30%	$ 3,260.87	$ 136.55

Enter the desired uptime level		99.999%	
		Loss Revenue	**Loss EBITA**
Number of outage hours per year	0.09	$ 950.22	$ 39.79
Number of outage minutes per year	5.25		

Figure 2.1

Of course we have to temper our excitement (you are excited aren't you?) with the realization that there is a cost associated with moving from the average downtime to the absolute minimum downtime. Five Nines has been proven to be unobtainable for some large organization with impressive resources. Carriers, for example, who have attempted to implement Five Nines, have found it to be an elusive goal, and will not commit to such a level in their service level agreements with even their largest customers. At Atrion, we prefer to aspire to the standards utilized by utilities. We refer to a network that achieves the highest practical level of operation as a Utility Grade Network (UGN). By practical we mean that the network is available and performing at optimal potential during critical operating hours. Where does that plug into our downtime calculator? That will vary per company. To my knowledge statistics that will provide downtime numbers for every particular scenario do not yet exist . Looking at the numbers in our examples is intended to be a wake-up call to action. It starts with the realization that you need to improve your view of the importance of IT. Assuming you agree, let's look at how to achieve optimal results.

We all have key employees in our companies. You know the people I'm talking about. The ones who literally make the company what it is. They are the leaders that others look up to. They are the ones you trust with major decisions. They are the ones you count on. Every company has them. It is just a question of how many of them you have, and how well you lead them, that determines the effectiveness, and ultimately the success of your organization.

Maybe it will help if we view your backbone network as a key employee that is critical to every company. As a play on the Utility Grade Network concept, let's call him eUGeNe. eUGeNe is your Utility Grade Network. In order to make it easier to read (and to type) for the remainder of this book I have replaced eUGeNe's full name with the acronym UGN, pronounced the very same way.

The statistics show that UGN is ill. He is bleeding. He has been neglected, and unappreciated, and even maliciously attacked. His keepers have been overworked and under-resourced, and in some cases are not really qualified to take care of him at all. In fact most people have very limited knowledge of how to take care of UGN.

That needs to change. Your business needs UGN. UGN needs to be healthy, happy, and well taken care of. UGN's overall health is your responsibility and he is counting on you. Your employees are counting on you to take good care of UGN, so he can perform well for them. Your customers will get very aggravated if you don't take care of UGN, causing him to slow down or flounder.

UGN has needs. In fact, much like all of your people. They have a set of needs identified long ago by Dr. Abraham Maslow, and commonly known as Maslow's Hierarchy of Needs, UGN has his own hierarchy of needs. We will spend the remainder of this book examining UGN's hierarchy of needs. UGN is such a critical employee in your organization that we are first going to assess how healthy he is. Then we are going to address each of his individual needs in detail. If you apply the proper attention to UGN and to meeting his needs, he will become one of, if not the, most valuable employee in your company.

Before we do, let's review Maslow's hierarchy in case you're not familiar with it, or fell asleep during that particular class...

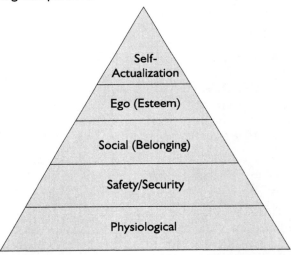

Maslow asserted that the most basic needs of an individual must be met before he can spend time or effort achieving the needs that exist on the next, higher level. On the most basic level are the needs for food and water for example. As one level of needs is reasonably satisfied, the individual is able to focus on the higher needs. At the highest level is the great wise man who is totally attuned to self and therefore able to achieve all that he can possibly achieve without fear or worry or doubt. I've explained it quite simply here, and this has been studied every way you can imagine. There are newer models that show additional levels. There are all kinds of behavioral approaches to a myriad of societal issues that stem from Maslow's assertions. There is no need to expound on them here. I simply want to invoke the same principle of building from very basic needs to higher needs, and therefore higher achievement, for our new friend UGN.

23

UGN's hierarchy of needs looks like this:

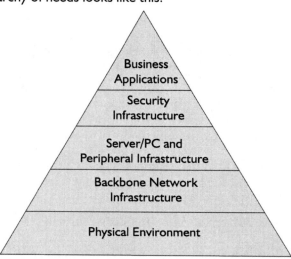

If you take this bottom up approach to building a utility grade network and ensure that all of the needs of each level are completely satisfied before moving up to the next level, what you will end up with is a network upon which the critical applications that your employees use every day to drive your business forward will perform at optimal levels at all times. UGN will thrive and become your best employee. He will give all of your other employees the potential to constantly perform at the optimum level. A serious flaw in any of the lower levels has the ability to bring the applications – and therefore the effective operation of your business – to a screeching halt.

More likely though, as shown in Chapter 1, UGN will have a constant stream of problems at the lower levels. These are issues that appear minor much of the time, like paper cuts. Have you seen how much paper cuts bleed sometimes? UGN's paper cuts bleed your money!

We will not spend time on the actual applications that run on your network. Those are as varied as the types of businesses that exist. We will take a look in detail at each of the supporting layers upon which those applications run. It is only in making the right investments into keeping UGN healthy at these lower levels that UGN is truly able to thrive at the highest level of strategic applications and provide the edge your company needs to thrive.

Physical Environment refers to the conditions of the locations where your IT equipment resides. In large organizations there is usually at least one raised floor computer room that provides a very clean and optimally conditioned environment. On the opposite end of the spectrum are places like the Connecticut company I mentioned earlier, where a storage closet is used to house the equipment so that it is out of the way. In such cases it is usually the same place where the phone company's circuits are terminated in the building. I can't tell you how many companies I have visited who stack expensive equipment on storage shelves or makeshift racks.

One of the favorites seems to be the strong metal wire racks that you often see in warehouses. I guess the idea is that the wire at least helps with air flow. Somewhere in between these two extremes is where you want to be if you are a small to mid-sized company.

Backbone Network Infrastructure, as discussed previously can, for the sake of discussing UGN's overall health, be viewed as just that, UGN's backbone. It is the conduit for his central nervous system. Have you ever listened intently to knowledgeable chiropractors? They will tell you that a perfectly aligned and healthy backbone is essential to good health. One disk slightly out of place can prevent a number of critical bodily functions from performing well. So it is with UGN's backbone. In this case it is made up of the network devices that are interconnected throughout your company to allow the efficient flow of information between communication devices. These communication devices include desktop and laptop computers inside and outside your company, phones, and the vast array of devices, from printers to barcode readers to blackberries, that rely on a healthy network to be effective.

Server/PC and Peripheral Infrastructure is both fairly self-explanatory and absolutely essential. These form UGN's brain and central nervous system. All the data is stored and disseminated from here. For the sake of this discussion it will include your data storage, backup, and recovery. A relative shared the story with me just yesterday of a young man who sustained a concussion in a football game. He has since gone on to experience short term memory loss, and even sporadic loss of vision. Doctors are attempting to determine exactly what is wrong and how to treat it. UGN experiences such trauma regularly if you are an average company. The forgotten data can be critical to your organization.

Security infrastructure refers to all of the measures that must be taken to ensure that your network and communication devices, as well as your server and desktop infrastructure and your physical infrastructure, are safe from either malicious attacks or unauthorized exposure. This goes beyond software and hardware and includes a comprehensive set of regulations and performance standards that are necessary to form a complete security plan. The unique thing about UGN as against other employees is that he is a constant target. Depending on your business this could be simply due to the fact that he exists, or because the knowledge he stores in his brain is extremely valuable to thieves or competitors. Regardless of why he is under attack, the security infrastructure you have around UGN is a critical need.

Beyond just the hierarchy of needs to keep UGN healthy, the approach that you take to satisfying those needs at every level is extremely important. There's a right way and a wrong way. Just putting the layers in place, even with the best equipment and technologies available, is not going to ensure you stop the bleeding. The right approach is to constantly combine the right technologies with your business objectives, and then take a complete life-cycle view of the technologies as you implement and support them.

One very valuable resource for aligning their business and the right technologies that smaller companies don't employ, and many larger ones do, is a Technology Council. (If you have jumped on the "alignment" bandwagon and have not seen the results you expected be sure to read the second paragraph of Chapter 7.) It sounds technical, but actually the majority of participants on the council should be from other areas than IT. We use a very similar model to drive decisions regarding the technologies that we invested in, and it has proven to be the very heart of our success. We formed a customer advisory board, comprised of a good cross section of our customers, who participated in very open and honest discussions regarding the technologies, services, and delivery mechanisms that our company needed to be proficient in to best serve their needs. Our success rate in introducing new technologies and new services improved dramatically.

That is exactly what you want your technology council to be and do. It should be a cross section of the people who use the technologies that are required to operate your business every day. The council should advise senior management and IT on a regular basis. It is pretty easy to get people to open up about what technologies will help them do their job better. You can also get honest feedback on how your current network and IT staff are performing. Lead the discussion in a positive, effective, and productive manner and you will learn a lot. You may invite customers to participate in the discussion if they rely on your IT to work with you. You should also invite the trusted advisor for IT that you have selected after you follow the guidelines in Chapter 5. There is so much going on in technology and it is sometimes easy to get wowed by new stuff. Focus is critical. Your technology council will help to keep your focus in the right places.

To achieve UGN status for the network that supports the decisions of your Technology Council it is necessary to examine the work patterns of your company in order to identify the most critical functions and their peak usage times. These functions must be configured to operate flawlessly during peak times. Then you must invest wisely, to reduce the risk of downtime. There are other functions that may be able to tolerate a slightly higher risk of downtime and less investment. Investing wisely means to tailor the solution and its level of resilience, and also the on-going support and response times associated with each solution.

UGN takes a lot of effort – but not a whole lot more effort than is required to build and maintain an average downtime network. If there was ever a case for working smarter versus working harder, this is it. UGN takes considerable planning to ensure that every dollar spent is going to directly impact productivity. The brightest CIOs that I have met, those who run multi-billion dollar organizations, all struggle to define and measure true return on IT investments. I can assure you of one vital fact: you will only experience the ROI on your investments in software applications if the entire network infrastructure on which they run is performing at peak levels at all times.

The life-cycle of your technology refers to the entire time the technology is employed to meet your business needs. It starts with planning and ends when the technology is replaced with something more effective.

We diagram the process of life-cycle support with a swirl which was actually incorporated into our logo years ago. A similar swirl or circle has since become the generally accepted practice for technology lifecycles in IT. I would hardly claim we invented it, but I can assure you that we have seen the very effective use of it first hand for a number of very loyal customers for many years. Here's our technology life-cycle methodology which you should adopt:

■ **Review**   ■**Assess**

■ **Support**   ■ **Implement**

■ **Train**

Assess. It is a never ending process that begins with assessing where you are. When your Technology Council decides you need a particular technology, or you realize that you need an upgrade to any portion of your infrastructure or need to add to it, your very first step is to determine the current condition of your network and possibility of incorporating the new technology into it. If you are one of the few companies that have precise, detailed documentation, this part should be relatively easy. If not, you'll want to hire an outside firm to do the assessment. In any case you need to thoroughly document the current state of your network in the process. You will need to analyze the impact of the new technology on existing performance, and you'll also need a full report on any other parts of the network that will need to be changed or upgraded in the implementation process to support the new technology. As mentioned in Chapter 1, a resource intense technology such as IP Telephony has a major impact on your existing network.

Implement. With the assessment in hand you can now work towards the next phase of the cycle, implementation. This is also the most complicated phase. It is impossible to overstress the planning phase of the implementation process. Things will go wrong during implementation. How prepared you are will determine how much these things will cost you in terms of money and manpower. Be prepared, you are going to bleed a bit here in all but the most rare cases. We are most often talking about intrusive surgery on UGN. The question is how badly and for how long. The assessment has a dramatic impact on the implementation and how painful it is. You can plan effectively based on the assessment. Planning effectively includes a detailed, documented project plan. I strongly suggest a team to construct and execute the project plan. The leader of the team must be a certified and experienced project manager with a proven track record. If you don't have one on your team, hire one. Another key person on the team is the Technical Director, who is someone with experience implementing the particular technology. Once again, if you don't have one on staff, hire one to work with your staff – and train your staff in the process, but we'll cover that in a moment. There should be a representative of the users of the technology on the team, and someone who will be responsible for the on-going support once the technology is up and running.

There was a time when you could get away with a well coordinated implementation. Those days are gone. Things are much too complicated now and are so interdependent that only a team approach with real project management will control the inevitable bleeding. The downtime in the UGN calculation at the beginning of this chapter is primarily planned, necessary downtime – unlike in the industry average calculation. With proper planning you'll be able to anticipate and control the downtime so that it has minimal impact on the operation of your company.

Train. With regard to training there are two important aspects. The first is the training of your IT staff. If this is the first time your staff has seen the technology I strongly suggest some introductory training before the technology is implemented. I am not in any way suggesting you do what most small companies do which is to send an IT person or persons to a training course on a new technology and then have them implement it on their network. That is the norm and it is just asking for trouble. I already stated that you need a technical director with prior experience in implementing the technology. The person with experience should also be required, during the implementation, to do some over-the-shoulder training for those unfamiliar with it, who will have to perform on-going support. The second aspect of training is that of the users of the new technology.

When large organizations implement new technology, thorough training of end users is often incorporated into the rollout. I have very seldom seen that happen in small- to medium-sized businesses. Most do some sort of training on how to use the new technology. I have found it to mostly be off the cuff and taught by some techno-geek (I can say that because I used to be one…) who assumes the audience would never understand the technical aspects of what is behind the device/application, what could go wrong with it, and what role the user could play in helping to reduce problems. Experience has taught me that the training should shed a little light on the technical aspects of what you are implementing. Stay away from acronyms unless they are so widely used that the user is likely to see them elsewhere. For example, most people have heard the term DSL in conjunction with high speed Internet into the home. They will feel like they just learned a big secret if you tell them it translates into Digital Subscriber Line simply because the line uses digital technology over the same subscriber line that has traditionally been used to carry voice conversations. Enough said. If your technical folks are like I was in my early days they would then go on to describe how the human voice is an analog signal with a curved wave form that operates in about a 3000hz frequency range. It runs through a series of filters and amplifiers that boost the signal as it travels along the line. If we replace these devices with digital square wave devices that actually recreate the signal – plausible because it is a square wave, we can send high speed data down that same circuit. Now, at what point did you drift off in the latter part of that training? I thought so. Most people would grab the basic DSL nugget and feel they just learned a lot about technology. Droning on beyond that causes them to tune out, makes them feel inferior, and adds another brick to the wall between your IT staff and general users. There are always exceptions, like the person who has a complex, blazing network in his/her home and runs game servers for an international group of interactive gamers. Do not try to teach to the exception. Don't let your techie get sidetracked with one of these people during the training. Insist they take it off-line.

Keeping the simple in mind, I also believe that your training should include some very basic troubleshooting and information gathering that users can perform should they run into trouble. Your objective is always to get the user back to full production mode as quickly as possible. To be clear, the bleeding I keep referring to is time when your users are not productive because your technology is not working properly. If they are able to provide some preliminary information to your technical support folks based on what they learned in training, it can dramatically reduce the time it takes them to become fully productive again. In addition, if they are equipped with some of the same language as your techies without needing to know exactly what it all means but just basically how it applies it can go a very long way towards building good relations – and eliminating the DAU label!

This is why I suggest that you do end-user training to reduce the mystery of technology for your employees – but strongly suggest that you sit through the presentation to make sure it is presented in a way that the average Joe can understand it. Of course, if you want the name of the aforementioned company, send me an e-mail – I'm sure they would gladly simplify your training, for a fee....

Support. Support for the technology, once implemented, is the only way to assure the optimal return on your investment. Only if the solution performs at peak levels at all times, is it really worth investing in. Your support strategy will vary depending on the size of your organization. We recognize and provide two important levels of support, pro-active and re-active. Pro-active support means real time monitoring of the technology that not only identifies if the equipment is working or not working, but also identifies if there are conditions that are affecting the performance of the technology without actually taking it down altogether. An example might be the workload of the processor in a server. You can't actually task a processor to 100 percent of its performance capacity without experiencing performance degradation. You see examples of this all the time when you open too many applications or websites on your PC at one time. You start to see delays. Pro-active monitoring tools can tell you if a similar condition is occurring in many different types of networking equipment. The more frequently this condition occurs the more likely that you need to invest in greater capacity to keep your users happy. With current pro-active monitoring tools you can personally be alerted by a variety of conditions on your network that may be performance impacting. I strongly suggest that you be in the loop. Most small to medium businesses find greater value in using an outside organization to perform pro-active monitoring due to simple economies of scale. The software to perform these functions is expensive, as is the talent to effectively use that software.

Re-active support is self explanatory. If you are utilizing pro-active support, you'll be alerted either by your staff or by a partner that a condition exists to which you must react. It may be a down condition that is already causing some bleeding or, as we discussed above, it may be something you need to react to in order prevent downtime. In either case someone must react. How quickly you are able to react also depends on a number of factors. If you are doing support in house it will depend on how well you are staffed and how qualified that staff is to diagnose and repair the problem. It will also depend upon how readily available a spare unit is if the problem is a failed piece of equipment. If you are depending on a support partner, the parameters of your contract with them determine how quickly they are required to react and how readily available they must make spare units. A spare unit is also not of much use if it is not pre-configured for the exact role that the existing unit is configured for. That is usually a function of archiving configurations for all devices on your network. This is no simple task, as we'll address in Chapter 7. How competent the partner's technicians are at reacting will depend largely upon how well you chose your partner. This is a topic to be discussed in Chapter 5.

The typical support scenario, whether conducted inside of your company, outside your company, or as a partnership, when an actual failure occurs, looks like this:

1) An alarm condition occurs which requires re-active support and it is immediately detected by your pro-active network management system. A trouble ticket is generated.

2) A re-active engineer immediately reacts by pulling up the most recent documentation on the hardware/software in question and remotely accessing the affected equipment and performing diagnostics. He closes or updates the trouble ticket based on his efforts.

3) If the problem cannot be solved remotely the trouble ticket is escalated and a technician is dispatched with a spare part in hand, along with detailed documentation that includes all entries in the trouble ticket. The dispatched technician repairs the alarm condition.

This should represent your worst case scenario – not your best. Your best case scenario is that your system identifies signs that a service affecting fault will occur only if some effective action is not taken in a timely manner. I would include scenarios where a fully redundant system has been implemented and the backup system is forced on line by a failure in the primary equipment. In that case the primary equipment is repaired or replaced and placed back on line, with little or no bleeding.

I assure you, these two scenarios are very different from what happens in most small- to medium-sized companies. End users usually identify an outage and IT does its best to react, usually dropping everything to do so if the outage is particularly severe. All the while your business is bleeding far more money than would have been the cost of putting the proper support structure in place ahead of time.

Review. The final phase of this lifecycle process involves the constant review of your technology. This also is multi-faceted. Here's what you should review and who should review it:

1. **Network Performance**. Should be reviewed on a quarterly basis by senior management. It should be a high-level report, viewed by senior management, that your pro-active monitoring tool or provider has supplied, and includes:

   a. General network performance and total downtime.

   b. The number of trouble tickets and mean time to resolve them.

   c. Any major outages affecting more than ten percent of users, number of users affected, duration of the outage.

   d. Existing conditions that require additional investment to prevent performance degradation.

   e. Any network security issues. We'll discuss this in greater detail in Chapter 9.

2. **User Satisfaction**. What gets measured gets attention. Measure this, and be sure senior management views the results every six months.

3. **Technology Advancements**. Your Technology Council should meet on a quarterly basis to discuss emerging technologies that could accelerate your company's performance.

If you design, implement, upgrade and support your network with UGN as your objective, the only time you should experience an outage is when you determine it is likely to have the least impact on your business. Try to imagine for a minute a fully redundant, resilient, self-healing network that is never not working when your employees are. There is no bleeding. That it is not a far stretch.

One final point involves important procedural issues.

Change management is critical to UGN. Whether it is to support new applications, to replace ageing equipment, or to install the inevitable updates in software, it has to be planned and executed properly. If that sounds time-consuming, consider that most of the changes on IT networks go poorly. The old saying "If I don't have time to do it right the first time, how in the world will I find the time to do it over?" definitely applies. Doing it over, after you have crippled the network, is never a good thing. How and when you implement change must be well thought out, clearly defined, and consistently enforced. That whole working smarter argument applies again. I can't tell you how many times I have seen scheduled upgrades not work out as planned.

My company does this every day for others and yet on our own network, a recent software upgrade caused some unanticipated issues that caused us to revert back to the previous revision. This was done in the middle of the night, on a weekend, with weeks of advanced notice. Going back was a simple issue, and our users experienced just a few minutes of additional time beyond the actual planned downtime for the upgrade, when that particular application was not available. Because of the chosen time, and the effective advanced planning – which included the possibility of aborting the changes, only two users were affected. When I address change management in Chapter 7, I'll expound upon what constitutes effective change management there.

Patches and fixes to the server vulnerabilities discussed in Chapter I are released on a regular basis. Each time a new fix is released it must be applied to each server running that particular operating system. The challenge is that there are all kinds of applications specifically written to run on these servers that may be adversely affected by the operating system's patch. There is a real science to keeping the servers current, so as not to leave them vulnerable, while not breaking any of the existing applications critical to your business that are running on these servers daily. This is definitely an area that must be handled by people who do it every day.

Connecting guests and new users to your network should not be taken lightly There are preventative measures you can take to ensure your individual users don't have a major impact on your network. Technology exists to examine devices thoroughly before they are allowed to connect to the general network. In many colleges a student is allowed to connect to the network but is isolated until their computer is scrubbed. The system can find and eliminate malicious software, and can upgrade various programs on the computer to enforce standards on the campus network. You may not need to take such strong measures on your own network, but you must certainly control who can connect, and what they can connect to your network. If you have guests who would benefit from being able to get out to the Internet while in your office, you can do so safely and easily without allowing them to get to any critical resources on your internal network. In the chapter on Network Access Control and Security, we'll look at these in some detail. With the recent proliferation of wireless networks this ability is generally expected.

These are just some of the more obvious procedural issues for keeping UGN healthy and well protected. More will come out and in greater detail in later chapters where we drill down into some of the details in each layer of UGN's hierarchy of needs. If you follow the advice in this chapter and wish to leave the rest to your staff you can basically stop reading now. Keep them accountable to the principles here, while providing the support and resources that it is within your control to provide, and you will see results. You will reduce the bleeding, or even stop it.

I respect that you are busy and don't have a lot of time for UGN. You probably don't have time to read this entire book. Chances are you are fortunate to have had the time to read this far. The last thing I want to do is waste your time.

If you want to drill down deeper, I have designed a quiz to save you time. Take the test in Chapter 3 to determine where UGN is healthy in your organization and where he needs attention. At the end of the book is the Answer Key. After you take the test, refer to the Answer Key to determine which chapters you need to read to go a bit deeper. It is that simple. Keep in mind we are not going to get down and dirty technical, but will keep the discussions at a more practical, strategic level. At the end of each chapter you will find a bulleted summary of the critical strategies, plans and documentation, and the investments you need to consider for that layer.

Chapter 3
The Test

This test is designed to help you assess the health of your own UGN. These are not technical questions, but practical ones centered on UGN's performance in your business. There are just 11 basic questions which you should be able to answer on your own, without input from your IT staff. They are multiple choice and you have the option of choosing "I don't know".

Once you have answered all 11 questions, please refer to the Answer Key in Appendix A.

1)   Which best describes your IT staff:

    a)   Extremely competent and effective

    b)   Competent and somewhat effective

    c)   Somewhat competent, not as effective as I would like

    d)   I don't know

2)   Which best describes your company's relationship with IT suppliers:

    a)   Strategic partnership

    b)   As needed consultants

    c)   Lowest bidder

    d)   I don't know

3) Which best describes your computer room:

    a) Conditioned, controlled, and protected power, temperature, humidity

    b) Air conditioned, reasonably clean and protected

    c) Converted closet/storage space, unprotected

    d) I don't know

4) Which best describes your IT equipment purchasing strategy:

    a) Standardized on key vendors in each critical area

    b) Somewhat standardized as budgets allow

    c) Lowest bidder

    d) I don't know

5) Which best describes the documentation available on your IT network:

    a) Current, complete, secure, and accessible to me

    b) Somewhat up to date and accessible

    c) Outdated and incomplete

    d) I don't know

6) Which best describes your e-mail and Internet connections:

    a) Robust and always available

    b) Always available but not always robust

    c) Sometimes unavailable and not often robust

    d) I don't know

7) Which best describes the performance of the most important software applications used to run your business:

    a) Robust and always available

    b) Always available but not always robust

    c) Sometimes unavailable and not often robust

    d) I don't know

8) How are you informed of critical outages or attacks on your network?
    a) I am automatically alerted instantly
    b) I am at the top end of an escalation procedure
    c) I know when I experience a problem myself
    d) I don't know

9) Which best describes your backup and disaster recovery plan:
    a) Well defined and regularly tested
    b) Minimally defined and tested
    c) Mostly on the fly
    d) I don't know

10) Which best describes your IT security policy:
    a) Well defined, communicated, and enforced
    b) Defined, loosely enforced
    c) We just use common sense
    d) I don't know

11) Which best defines your overall opinion regarding IT:
    a) Provides an important strategic advantage for the investments made
    b) Is necessary for daily operations but provides few strategic advantages
    c) Very expensive with limited ROI
    d) A constant source of frustration.

Thank you, please go to Appendix A at this time.

Chapter 4
IT Staff

Technical people are hard to come by, and they often share some if not all of these characteristics:

◆ They are jacks of all trades and masters of one. Yes, I meant to leave off the first "n". Most technicians have a particular area of expertise. They have mastered one particular aspect of technology. It may be servers and operating systems, it may be switches and routers, it may be security and firewalls...the list goes on and on. It takes masters to keep your UGN healthy. If your folks are masters of particular areas of technology-and I hope for your sake they are, they need help in the areas where they are not.

◆ Another characteristic is that they are often not willing to admit they need help. This is often the fault of management who assumes they know everything about IT, and who don't understand the complexities of it and the need to specialize. Would you have a podiatrist perform your bypass? Here, by the way, is where much of the difficulty lies in terms of establishing a trusted advisor relationship with an outside vendor, a relationship that you cannot do without. Your people need to be secure enough to be able to admit what they don't know and to get the help they need. I will get to that in Chapter 5.

◆ They are often poor communicators. Even if they have good written or oral skills, which mean they are the exception, they will struggle with the jargon issues we discussed in the first chapter.

◆ They are overworked. Technology is not only their job, it is their hobby. Therefore, they spend countless hours on the web, working on the side, gaming or building their own home network. Even if you aren't burning their candle at both ends, they are. They are just that type of people.

◆ They tend to do a poor job of documenting what they have done.

♦ They are often introverts.

♦ And finally, they are mostly tactical, rather than strategic, thinkers. The NeverFail study regarding e-mail downtime, also uncovered this truth. The study found that there is a disconnect between acceptable levels of downtime. IT sees it one way. The business sees it differently. "It's ... like (there is) this disconnect between what IT thinks is an acceptable level of service and what business requires," Barnes said, adding that, in some cases, IT departments believe it's acceptable to be e-mail-less for four hours. "When businesses rely on e-mail communication for their livelihoods, that four hours could be disastrous."

Many of the technicians I've met over the years don't fully understand the direct correlation between idle workers and the resulting hit to profits...come to think of it, a lot of business owners don't get it. You, however, are different. You get it, or at least want to. That's why you're still reading...

With all that said, the biggest problem we face in the IT industry is a lack of qualified people. The situation is getting worse before it gets better. Bureau of Labor statistics in the US indicate a 12% decrease in computer repair technicians since 2001. This is the very time when technology is evolving at an extremely rapid pace and becoming far more critical to your company. Part of the reason was revealed to me in a recent conversation I had with an enterprising young man. He works in a factory. He is bright and articulate and enjoys using technology, so I had to ask why he doesn't do it for a living. He pointed to another guy at his factory who has a four-year degree in Computer Science. He said the guy couldn't seem to get an entry level job because the stuff he learned in school was outdated in the marketplace. His conclusion: IT as a field is just too difficult to break into and to stay current in. It is just not worth all that effort for what it pays. Of course, the pay scale he looked at was entry level. I explained that once he did break in the income potential was tremendous. As we ended the conversation I could tell he was not convinced. If that is the general consensus of our youth, the problem is only going to get worse. Those who are in the field know this. That continues to drive pay up. US companies looking to hire skilled IT professionals will pay, on average, 5.3 percent more in 2008 than they did in 2007, according to the Robert Half Technology's 2008 IT Salary Guide released in December of 2007. This is almost twice the US consumer index. A January 2008 study of employment figures shows the IT industry at full employment.[1]

The situation in the UK isn't any better. A September 2007 article at computing. co.uk provided the cold hard facts: The UK IT industry is growing five to eight times faster than other sectors and needs 150,000 new entrants each year. The number of students choosing IT-related degrees sank from 27,000 to 14,700 between 2001 and 2005. At the same time mathematics and computer sciences showed the highest university dropout rate in the UK, with one in ten undergraduates not continuing into a second year of study, according to the National Audit Office. Within the

---

[1] The actual unemployment rate according to US Bureau of Statistics is 2.1, which economists consider full employment

existing workforce IT leaders report a lack of relevant skills as the sector becomes increasingly aligned with the business. Even still a comprehensive study by the UK IT recruitment specialist CV Screen released in May of 2007 found that permanent IT salaries had risen by 5.5% in the previous 12 months.

It is no wonder you are frustrated by the whole IT situation. The information we've presented so far can be summed up to conclude that if you are an average company your IT department doesn't understand your business, thinks it is doing a better job than everyone else in your company thinks it is doing, does not like to communicate with you and when it does it tends to talk in language you can't understand – and then tends to make you feel inferior for not understanding. Most of the technology they deliver underperforms and goes over budget. While all of this is going on the staff continue to demand higher pay, fall behind new technologies, do a very poor job of documenting what they have done, and then tend to leave you within a two- to three-year time period to fend for yourself with this poorly documented mess they have created. When they do leave, they tend to leave for much higher pay. Don't blame me, I'm just the messenger. These are documented facts. And these facts are costing you big money as we saw in Chapter 1. So who is to blame? You.

You are always to blame because the buck stops with you. You have preferred to ignore the problem, or delegate, or rope your brother/cousin/uncle into dealing with it. You know I'm not making this up. Frank Shaw, Foresight Director at independent UK think-tank the Centre for Future Studies , says the vast majority of SMEs do not have adequate technology expertise. "A number of firms we looked at relied on friends and family for IT advice." The definition of insanity is doing the same thing over and over and expecting different results.

I've already said much of this, but I repeat it here so you recognize that, with these attributes, you will not get what you need out of IT unless you force the issue. Look at these combined attributes. Do you think they make for a largely happy crowd? Add to all of this, that they are under constant and ever increasing pressure. Does all this make you feel bad that you haven't paid more attention to these folks, especially considering that they work their butts off to keep your network going? You should. And you should give them some relief. Here is how you do it. Sit them down, tell them that you now have a clue of what they are up against, and that you are not only going to take a greater interest in what they are doing, but that you are going to give them the resources they need, the recognition they deserve, and that you are going to get them some help. That will put a smile on their faces. Then also let them know the help is going to come from outside the organization, and that you are not only going to expect the network to be up most of the time, you are going to personally monitor it to make sure that it is. Of course that may wipe those smiles off!

If you have the money to place a competent person in charge of IT, there are attributes that this person must possess if he or she is going to lead in a way that is effective for your business. In large companies these are the attributes of the Chief Information Officer. In medium companies they are usually the traits of the IT Manager. In small companies they are very seldom the traits of the IT guy. I say the

IT guy because studies also report that in many small to medium businesses there is a single person responsible for all IT related tasks. For larger SMEs in the 200+ employee range Shaw says; "Their main deficiency tends to be in IT management skills generally. They have not related their technological capability to their strategic objectives and planning."

I'll address small to medium businesses in this book since that is our focus. Most IT managers and IT guys have risen to the position after having done most of the IT work and built up a staff as the company has grown (assuming the company has grown). Look at whoever is leading your IT efforts and take stock of the attributes that he or she brings to the table. An interesting side note on this issue is that the Society of Information Management's 2008 list of 30 books that IT leaders absolutely must read contained just one book that had anything to do at all with technology. The best IT leaders should have some combination of a number of the following attributes:

1) A passionate desire and ability to understand your business, your strategy, and your value to your customers.

2) An understanding of the economic engine that drives the profitability of your business.

3) Humility.

4) Integrity.

5) Vision.

6) A clear ability to communicate effectively both verbally and in writing.

7) An understanding and successful record of overseeing IT Project Management.

8) Detailed knowledge and ability in at least one area of technology.

9) Strong vendor relationships.

10) A team oriented work history.

11) Rock solid references.

It is no accident that the majority of these attributes have a lot more to do with non-technical skills than with technical skills. The most effective companies have the most effective IT led by the most effective managers. It doesn't matter if the people they are managing are on your staff, or are people they trust outside of your company. Let's expound a bit on these before we talk about the people they trust outside of the company, the trusted advisors, in the next chapter.

The first two attributes are the ones least understood as IT leadership attributes. This is where your thinking changes if you currently view IT as a necessary expense. It is a necessary expense, no doubt about it. IT is both necessary, and expensive; all the more reason for doing it right. The person who leads your IT efforts has to start with the roadmap of your business. How did your business get where it is? Where are you going and why? What will it take to get there? How can IT support or even accelerate that plan?

He must also know exactly how you make money. What are the critical activities that produce profit for your company (your economic engine)? Remember Activity Based Costing in your managerial accounting classes? If your IT manager doesn't understand that concept and how it pertains to your business, you need to fix that. If you're bringing someone new in, he must understand it. I've done some general business consulting that was not centered on IT and in every case I have started there; what activities make the most money for your business, followed by how can you do more of them, and less of everything else? Your IT manager must understand that and then look at the ways in which technology can enhance those activities. The only way that he can be an effective member of your technology council is if he is armed with this knowledge.

The next three attributes pertain to every hire in our company and should for yours as well. By humility I do not mean that he should be a wimp. Quite the contrary. He should be extremely confident in his ability to get the job done. It is important that he not be conceded and boastful about it. Cocky technicians tend to intimidate others with their knowledge and have a real hard time relating to those who don't know what they know. I am not implying that it is easy to find this combination of attributes in anyone, let alone in a technical person. I will say that in my experience, integrity is a very common attribute in technical folks. Sometimes they are honest to a fault, so the communication skills are also quite critical. These attributes are a bit of a challenge to measure. It may take a personality profile, which is fairly common these days for companies that are determined to hire only the best candidates who will fit into their business culture. If you need more information, there are countless books on the subject and I'll once again defer to the book *Good to Great*. Get the right people on your bus. Every one of them must have these three attributes. We have had tremendous success in this area, and I will tell you exactly how a little further into this chapter.

Communication skills, attribute 6, is a tough one for many technical people, as I have mentioned. This position requires it. If you are interviewing, insist on a presentation on the technology that the candidate is most familiar with. Can he put it in layman's terms? Is he passionate about it? You should see a clear and articulate understanding of the technology, communicated in easy to understand terminology, and sprinkled with a clear vision of where the technology is going, and how it might benefit your organization. We've had real success with those who can do this type of presentation well, regardless of the position they are being hired for. If you've been in the habit of hiring people without a great deal of work up front and hoping for the best, you'll need to adjust that for filling this position. Understand that the concepts of this book, and achieving the results that you need, will only be possible if the right person is driving the entire process. You may have the right person in that position already, and if so that is wonderful. You may instead have someone with the negative attributes I've described and need to make an adjustment. Or you may not have anyone in the role of leading IT and see the critical importance of that position now, since you do intend to get IT performing as the strategic asset that it should be for your company. Whatever the case, you'll need to assure that the right person in charge of your IT is one who has these attributes. Let's continue down the list…

Success in Project Management can mean that the person has experience working on successful projects as a project manager himself, or that he has led successful managed projects from the technical side, the vendor side, or the customer side. Even the smallest implementations of technology benefit greatly from project management. Putting the project plan together as an exercise itself requires clearly defining the steps and the resources required to complete the implementation. We will discuss this in detail when we look at the implementation of technology in the next section.

Remember that most technical people are jacks of all trades, master of one. The one is extremely important. It really makes little difference what the one thing they master is, as long as it is directly related to Internet-working. Technologies are so interrelated that if he is a true expert in any one technology, it is very likely he is pretty competent in related technologies as well. Having a very strong understanding in one area as I have stated, doesn't mean that he is an expert in every area. Back to the humility thing again – a good candidate knows what he doesn't know and readily admits it. This is why the ability to forge strong vendor relationships, attribute 9, is critical.

Look for someone who has served on advisory boards for vendors. Almost any client using a technology or an integration firm is invited to serve on an advisory committee or a user group or a similar group. This says a lot about the individual. It typically means that he is very committed to the solution(s) provided by the vendor, wants to know everything he possibly can about the solution(s) and the vendor, and wants to have some say in the future advancement of the vendor and the vendor's solutions. It usually leads to some great contacts in the industry. A recent study showed that those who participate in user groups are more successful in implementing technologies, and find that the time invested is well worth the effort. When you look at the four quadrants of time management, participation in these groups demonstrates the ability and the desire to function in Quadrant 2.

If there is one thing critical to the future of your network it is the ability of your IT leader to function in Quadrant 2.

In case you are unfamiliar with the Quadrants of time management they are shown here in Figure 4.1. Most of us in IT have no choice but to spend the majority of our time in firefighting mode, addressing what is urgent and important. In order to plan effectively, however, we must spend time in Quadrant 2 doing the important research on new technologies, examining their significance and ability to enhance the objectives of our business, and determining how they can be incorporated into the network and effectively supported for the life-cycle of the technology. Any time in Quadrants 3 and 4 is just not acceptable.

	URGENT	NOT URGENT
NOT IMPORTANT	QUADRANT 1	QUADRANT 2 QUALITY TIME
IMPORTANT	QUADRANT 3 DISTRACTION	QUADRANT 4 TIME WASTING

Figure 4.1: The quadrants of time management

A lot has been made of the concept of teams. The subject has been examined every which way, and the definition of team tends to vary depending on who you talk to. When it comes to IT you need a high performance team. One characteristic of techies is that they are often loners. I've seen many who hoard information and protect their own knowledge in the name of job security. Nothing will create more conflict in your IT department, where you have all these masters of one technology who must interact with other masters on a regular basis. When these masters have a team approach and readily share information so that all rise in knowledge and ability it is truly a beautiful thing to watch. We had just such a team at Atrion when we achieved our first direct certification as a Cisco Silver Partner. It took many individual certifications to make the company certified. The group took a team approach with everyone helping each other to study, practice in the lab, and take the tests. Now many of those same people bring that level of dedication to designing and implementing networks for our customers. When we walk into a business with a team approach that also works well, the two teams blend smoothly. When we run into lone soldiers, an inevitable battle ensues. Egos start to inflate as people insist on doing things their way. We do all we can do to overcome that, and are usually successful.

Occasionally though, it is an extremely difficult engagement and our folks get battered in the process. No team is ever perfect, but a solid, high performance team will not only work together well, but will quickly isolate a lone soldier and push him out. Your leader needs to be someone who has successfully worked on a high performance team. You can profile for that, but you'll need to rely on what they describe in the interview process when you ask them what teams they have been a part of, what the team was able to accomplish and what the best and the most challenging aspects of working on that/those team(s) was. You'll have to confirm that all with solid references.

References are a bit hard to come by these days. Privacy policies and lawsuits have made getting references a challenge. I tend to believe that if they can't give me a real down to earth person that has been on a team with them and is willing to share the details openly I am just not interested. Maybe the reference is not inside their existing company or even a company they have directly worked for. It may be a solid reference from a vendor who mobilized a team at their company to complete a successful project implementation. Wherever you get the reference, you need to get it.

It may seem like such a person doesn't exist. I assure you I know a lot of people who fit this description perfectly and I've had the pleasure of working with many of them for years. I have also encountered many people over the years who had some of these characteristics and acquired the others along the way. The attribute of humility usually means that they are both teachable, and willing to step out of their comfort zone for the greater good. With a very specific plan to do so, we have been fortunate to build a solid team that includes a whole bunch of people like this. I'll give you a glimpse into how we have done it. I say this not to blow my own horn. In fact, it is the people who work at my company who have done this. One indisputable fact is that good people attract good people. Early on we made some very good hiring decisions, and some very bad ones. The good ones, fortunately, stayed and attracted more good ones. They are the ones who formulated this methodology because they benefit with every good hire, and suffer through every bad one. If you have less than stellar people do not hesitate for one second to open up their employment opportunities. The good ones will thank you for it, and wonder what took you so long.

Here is some of what we do:

Interview Process

We incorporate a multi-layer interviewing process for potential candidates, and during the interview a candidate will meet separately with three to five interviewers. Each interviewer will ask a predetermined list of standard interview questions which are used to gauge if the candidate shares our values on honesty, integrity, and client service. We have established a minimum requirement that all candidates must undergo at least two interview cycles. Once the candidate has been identified for employment, our Human Resources department will complete an employment history verification as well as reference checking.

Background Screening

We use an outside company to perform more in depth background screening. All potential new employees are subjected to background checks. We conduct a multi-county criminal history report including seven- to ten-year felony and misdemeanor searches for all open and closed cases by all names identified on the employment application as well as any nicknames, maiden names, aliases, and/or diminutives derived during the screening process. If a candidate refuses to have a background check conducted they become ineligible for employment. In addition, we use an outside company for social security number verification. On an as needed basis, we will also perform motor vehicle background checks for employees who will be using their personal vehicles to routinely travel to client locations.

Psychometric Testing

We use psychometric testing from an outside firm to focus on understanding a candidate's personal interests, attitudes, and values. Combined with our interview process and background screening, we gain an understanding of an individual's attitudes which help to ascertain why they do things. A review of an individual's experiences, references, education, and training helps to determine their capabilities. Behavioral assessments help to tell us how a person behaves and performs in the work environment. The Psychometric Report measures the relative prominence of six basic interests or attitudes (a way of valuing life): Theoretical, Utilitarian, Aesthetic, Social, Individualistic and Traditional. Attitudes help to initiate one's behavior and are sometimes called the hidden motivators because they are not always readily observed especially during an interview process. It is the purpose of this analysis to help illuminate and amplify some of those motivating factors and to build on the strengths that each candidate brings to the work environment.

Confidentiality Agreement

Our Human Resources department maintains an Employee Handbook that contains our employment policies related to employee conduct, hiring and firing practices, employee benefits, and security information. Deviations from the Code of Conduct detailed in the Employee Handbook are investigated and responded to by management. Consequences of Code of Conduct violations can include termination. Due to the nature of the information that our employees will have access to, new employees are counseled about the confidential nature of the information and are required to sign a confidentiality agreement as a condition of employment. Unless it has specifically been designated as public, all internal information must be protected from disclosure to third parties.

Notice that there isn't a lot of detail here regarding technical competence. There doesn't have to be. The people they are going to work with interview them. They can't bluff their way in. We look for that "master of one" attribute for technical employees. We'll cross train them in what they don't know. And it will be a pleasure to do so because we will have already determined that they are highly competent, self motivated, with a great attitude and the ability to work with others.

If you have a very small department and they don't have the mastery of the particular skill you are hiring for, and therefore can't test prospective employees, do what one of my best customers has done over the years – ask for help from outside your company. As we've already discussed, and will greatly expound on in the next chapter, you need to have go-to people outside of your company. If they are a true partner they will be willing to do whatever it takes to help you, and that may include spending hours interviewing your potential candidates.

One last point. In case you're thinking that you should just outsource your entire IT function, and thus not have to worry about it, you should recognize that sixty eight percent of companies surveyed in March of 2007 found outsourcing to be overrated as an IT cost cutting strategy and sixty seven percent identified the total cost of using domestic outsourcing vendors as being more expensive than doing the same work in house. In won't save you money, and you will have less control. I believe a much wiser strategy is to right-source, which means using in-house staff where you have the competency – and for IT leadership, then augmenting that staff with outside help.

Chapter 5
Build Trust Outside of Your Company

No one can know everything. Your IT folks will have specific areas of expertise as we discussed in the last chapter. You can't afford to keep on staff all the people with all the expertise in each particular technology that forms your total solution. But a solution designed by one person is most likely to be less effective than it could be. The level of knowledge and experience required to integrate technology effectively is extensive regardless of the size of your company. I have yet to encounter a company that has unlimited resources. It is specifically the limit of your resources that requires you to work with a company or companies you can trust to provide the information and advice you need, and to provide competent people to augment your existing staff.

I want to be clear that I am not talking about a vendor who provides a single product and helps to integrate their product into your network. You made need that at times. I am advocating a long term partnership with a company that provides a number of the solutions you need, and is competent and trustworthy enough to be the focal point for all of your projects, even if they have to partner with other firms to provide the entire solution. More about that further down.

One very valuable resource that smaller companies don't employ, and many larger ones do, is a Technology Council. It sounds technical, but actually the majority of participants on the council should be from other areas besides IT. We used a very similar model to drive decisions regarding the technologies that we invested in and it has proven to be the very heart of our success. We formed a customer advisory board, comprised of a good cross section of our customers, who participated in very open and honest discussions regarding the technologies, services, and delivery mechanisms that our company needed to be proficient in to best serve their needs. Our success rate in introducing new technologies and new services improved dramatically.

That is exactly what you want your technology council to be and do. It should be a cross section of the people who use the technologies that are required to operate your business every day. The council should advise senior management and IT on a regular basis. It is pretty easy to get people to open up about what technologies will help them do their job better. You can get honest feedback on how your current network and IT staff are performing. Lead the discussion in a positive, effective, and productive manner and you will learn a lot. You may invite customers to participate in the discussion if they rely on your IT in order to work with you on a regular basis. You should also invite the trusted advisor for IT that you have selected after you follow the guidelines later in this chapter. There is so much going on in technology and it is easy to get wowed by new stuff. Focus is critical. Your technology council will help to keep your focus in the right places.

I recently read an interesting book called *Freakonomics*. One particular point they make has to do with knowledge, and the effective transfer of knowledge. The main theme of the second chapter was asymmetrical communication. They concluded that most businesses gain great advantage through the hoarding of information, which they cleverly dole out to their clients for large fees. They point to real estate agents (in a particularly unflattering way I might add) and insurance agents. The examples used in the book; real estate and insurance, are not anywhere near as complex as the business of running the IT systems that businesses need. I point this out to say that the cost of technology integration performed by the right people at the right time in the right way is actually a tremendous value, has far more daily impact on your business, and will heavily affect the bottom line. Inside companies I have often seen this hoarding of information used by technicians under the guise of job security. While the cost of technology is high, information regarding which technologies will help you, and which ones will not, is a major part of the value equation when engaging a trusted advisor and in forming your Technology Council. Still you are skeptical…

At a recent conference I attended, the speaker from a research firm in New York called AMI Partners indicated that one of the major inhibitors to relationships between your business and a value added partner is a lack of trust. You believe that giving up control or management of any part of your Information Technology solution is risky and that you can do it more economically in-house. You are right in both regards. There is risk in going outside of your company. If your staff has a lot of knowledge and experience in a particular area of technology, implementing the solution will be cheaper using your staff. To have your staff support it is another story. That will cost you more in-house. Part of the fear is actually based on past experiences. Part of it is just the incredible resistance to change discussed in Change or Die. Listen, there are approximately 239,000 solution providers in the US alone. Just because you've had a bad experience, or even a couple of bad experiences, doesn't mean there are not partners out there that you can trust. It simply means that you have to take a more active role in investigating who you partner with to find just the right fit. Just as you damage your business every time you make a bad hire – and bad hires are your fault – you really damage your business when you choose a bad outside partner. You need a partner, and you must find the perfect partner for your business. Once you do, it must truly be a partnership.

IT systems integrators have a lot of knowledge that you don't have. IT is a knowledge-based business. The technology changes so quickly that unless you are in the technology business specifically, you cannot possibly stay abreast of what is best for your company. However, an integrator is only going to know what new technologies are right for your business if they know your business, and your network, inside out. This comes with time. The time it takes can be shortened by participation on your technology council. It can also be shortened if, once you choose a trusted partner, you hire them to do a complete assessment of what you have, the documentation you have, and the processes in place for implementations, change management, security, and support.

There is no doubt that a technician who spends every day integrating solutions into other companies' networks (as network integrators do) is eventually going to get good enough to integrate that solution into pretty much any environment. It does become as much an art as a science. Still, he is at a distinct disadvantage if he has never seen your network prior to this implementation. To be sure, there is always a first time, but if every time a technician installs a new solution on your network it is the first time, the chances of success are severely diminished.

> **Side note:** *I use "he" and "his" only because there are an overwhelming majority of technicians who are male. Our company has sponsored and participated in many events to encourage, highlight, and support women in technology. Ladies, technology is a great field, it pays well, and your intellect will be highly respected. Ask any women who is in it —my experience is that they seem to generally be the happiest technicians!*

I have found, over the years, two opposite types of customer who have employed my company and other network integrators. The first are those who trust no-one but themselves, insist on hiring the lowest bidder, treat their integrator as an adversary who is trying to take advantage of them, and then try to take advantage of the integrator as often as possible. Interestingly, organizations with this attitude regularly hire high-priced consulting firms. That still confuses me, but I dare not speculate as to why that is.

The second are those who consider the integrator a trusted partner, establish a long term relationship, and treat them as a true partner.

In twenty years I have never once seen the first type of client thrive. Even if their company somehow manages to do well despite their IT department, these types of companies have constant problems, incredible turnover, and everyone in the IT community eventually catches on to their mode of operation, so that only the least qualified and experienced vendors bid on their project, usually then end up losing money, and vow never to deal with them again. You'd think they might catch on to their own folly. Not true. I can count on one hand the number of such clients who eventually turned around, saw the light, and began to do things right. When they have, however, the transformation has been dramatic.

More often than not, it is the IT manager who conducts him/herself in this way, with senior management, or company owners, either not realizing what is going on, or turning a blind eye to it. That is just not acceptable any more. The buck has to stop squarely on the desk of the leaders – who must know exactly what is going on.

I try to stay away from "never" and "always" because they are seldom accurate. Not all customers are on either of these extremes. Many fall somewhere in the middle. So their networks are only partially screwed up. These people are lukewarm, not really committed to doing things with excellence, but subscribing to an attitude that is willing to settle. And settle they do. These are the folks who are largely responsible for the dramatic downtime statistics in Chapter 1. Lukewarm is just unacceptable to describe anything but baby's bathwater.

You have to adopt an attitude of passion for the performance of your technology systems. I don't have to make that case. Businesses that use technology effectively outpace the competition by leaps and bounds. (If you want to understand what I mean by using technology effectively in this case, read the last chapter of Jim Collin's book *Good to Great*.) This is a commonly understood and accepted fact. Yet even these companies who deploy the latest technologies fall into the average downtime category in most cases. When you take a passionate position regarding your network systems, you have to consider the importance of a competent trusted partner.

Why is this trusted partner so critical? How do you know who you can trust? What does this relationship look like? Allow me to tell you.

A good trusted partner in information technology is likely to be a solid, reputable integration firm with technical sales people. A technical salesperson has the ability to discuss the most technical solutions in laymen's term from a strategic perspective. If he is with the right company he also has a solid team behind him who can go deeper into the technical details of the solutions that will drive your business forward. You may very well already be dealing with an organization that has the potential to truly step up and be your trusted partner. If you are not sure, then you need to assess the firm(s) you are doing business with today. I realize that this may be something you have delegated to a subordinate. Your own IT folks may have purposely built a wall between you and them. Before I discuss how to recognize the right firm, I want to assure you that the transition from an arms-length relationship to a trusted partner relationship, if you have the right integrator, will not be that difficult. I've seen very poor relationships turn around under the right circumstances. It is up to you to create the right circumstances. One of the starkest examples I have experienced occurred somewhat by accident, but illustrates that change is both very possible and very beneficial to all involved.

In the very early days of Atrion we dealt with a company that had a reputation for shopping – which translates into always choosing the lowest bidder and then squeezing the life out of whoever did business with them. Of course, I was quite sure that with exceptional service I could change all that. We installed a few different solutions over a period of about ten years.. The client never bought any type of service contract, even though they always bought the solution for the absolute lowest price. We made precious little profit margin, and in fact I often had to go to the manufacturers of the products we provided and work with them to get some additional discount so we could make even the smallest profit. One of the lessons about business that I had not yet learned was that there really is such a thing as bad business. Not surprisingly this customers' network was plagued with more than its share of problems. The IT manager was a tough guy to deal with, but always pleaded for help saying that he had no choice but to go with the lowest bidder, since upper management made him do it. I truly felt bad for the guy and got into the habit of jumping to help his company whenever there was a problem. I was not completely unselfish since I believed that I was sure to get preferred treatment when the next opportunity came along. I even fixed problems that had nothing to do with the work that we had done. A couple of times I remember fixing shoddy work done by a competitor – again thinking that might earn me some brownie points on the next deal, or at least some respect.

The trouble is that I began hearing that the client was telling my competition that his network problems were the result of doing business with my company. That was troubling. Even our friendly rivals were questioning what we were doing wrong there, since our reputation was stellar. The only thing I could figure is that this guy really was clueless, and couldn't differentiate between our work and the work of others. I also thought that perhaps because I had the audacity to actually fix problems left by other vendors – mostly the types of competitors that came and went – and never really became part of the community of IT solution providers, (I've found that this type of community inevitably forms in any area where there are competent competitors who compete respectfully with each other) he somehow associated those problems with me.

Another issue that bugged me even more was that I was very active in the local community on a lot of levels and I had opportunities to interact with his boss. The guy seemed to have very little respect for me or my company. He was cordial but I could sense something very wrong. When a very large project came up, the largest that they had undertaken since I had known them, we barely got the time of day. They chose another vendor. It was common knowledge that this vendor had been having a lot of trouble with the particular technology that was being implemented. My company, on the other hand, was developing a great reputation in that area. Since we were both representing the same manufacturer's product, the manufacturer wanted us to get the deal, because they knew it would reflect more positively upon their products and image. We did everything we could, and yet we lost the deal.

Adding insult to injury was the fact that just months before I had personally responded to an outage. I had not been in the field for a long time, but they had a problem with some older equipment that I was well versed in. I went out personally on the call. Get this: my service department wouldn't go out on the call because the customer was not willing to pay for the call, and had made us wait months and months and even disputed the bill for the last time we had dropped everything to fix this clients problem. Tell me this is not a well-managed company....!! Still, not bright enough to know when to say no, I circumvented my own system. I fixed the guy's problem and sent him no bill. He seemed, for once, to really appreciate my efforts. So when I heard that the deal went to the less qualified competitor, it hurt.

Not nearly as much though, as when I found out from the manufacturer, that the client's senior management had indicated that they had done business with us for years and were very disappointed with the results. They had been told by our direct contact in their organization, that the real source of years of problems with their network was the fact that they had purchased many of their solutions from Atrion. The same guy I had helped for all of the these years without a service contract and without getting a dime in most instances, had been throwing us under the bus for all the problems with his hodgepodge of a network that he had thrown together with low-bid competitors. If you are a dedicated, trustworthy integrator or have ever worked for one you can probably relate to this incredible story. Have faith, there is a happy ending...

The low bidder on the major project did a pretty lousy job. The manufacturer had to do a lot of work to clean things up. The company decided they needed a service contract since this technology was critical to their daily operation. The manufacturer strongly suggested that they consider us. This provided the one opportunity I had been waiting for for almost 20 years; I had the opportunity to meet with the CIO and the CFO. The purpose of the meeting was for us to defend our response to their Request for Proposal (RFP). In the past, the IT manager had simply verbally asked for a written price quote. This time, the company had sent out an actual written RFP. This was going to be a strategic meeting.

I finally got the opportunity to sit in front of the guys that the IT Manager had blamed all his problems on for years. Remember, they made him choose the low bidder. And they were finally going to get the opportunity to hammer the guy that their IT guy for years had blamed all his network problems on. Talk about a hot seat!

Of course, within minutes we found, as usually happens, that the most senior people in both organizations were pretty good people, very open, and very approachable. We hit it off well and talked about a lot of things that had nothing to do with IT. Then we got down to business. They indicated that our price was a bit high. Aha, some truth to the IT guy's assertions. I indicated that you get what you pay for. But I also had a couple of questions, because we are very specific to design our solutions to exactly meet the client's needs. Perhaps there were aspects of the RFP that were a bit more than they really needed. If so, we could custom tailor the solution, and maybe shave off a little cost in the process. I started asking strategic questions. What exactly was the business reason for investing in the technology in the first place? How was the technology either living up to its potential, or not doing so on a day-to-day basis? What are the most critical times for this technology to perform at peak efficiency? Are there times when the solution has no bearing on company performance? As the discussions went on, it actually became apparent that, although the RFP specified a low-cost, reactive support agreement, with significant delays in response in order to keep the costs down, what the client was experiencing was a huge monetary loss for specific times when the technology was most critical, but had failed completely. We discussed ways to ensure that the technology was always ready for those critical times. At the end of the day, the customer purchased a much more robust, custom-tailored, pro-active support solution. It was more expensive than the RFP response. Not a lot more though, and in their CFO's eyes, a tremendous value for the accompanying performance assurance. They, and we, have been very happy partners since. What about that IT manager? Believe it or not, he is ecstatic! We did for him, in one strategic meeting, what he had been unable to do, for whatever reason, for his entire career at this firm. It was like years of tension just evaporated. We became his trusted advisor. Don't you love a happy ending?!

There is no better story to illustrate the difference between the arm's length relationship, and that of a trusted partner. The added benefit, besides all of the business benefits, is that the relationship is fun, it is pleasant. It is, to use a highly overworked phrase, a win-win relationship. I believe that every business requires just such a relationship. Of course, getting back to the *Freakonomics* viewpoint, cynics might believe that I have a vested interest in trying to convince you of this point. I suppose that could be true if your company is in the New England region of the US and decides to contact my company for help with your networking solutions. We cover the six New England states – and I have four of our five kids currently in college. So if you are in our area please don't resist the urge to call! ;o) If not, I get only the satisfaction of knowing your business will benefit tremendously if you follow this advice. We do belong to a nationwide group of like-minded systems integrators in the US, who share advice and best practices called INService. I would not likely derive any benefit if you are a US firm and use our group to find a trusted partner, but my friends in those businesses might owe me a dinner. Their website is www.INService.org . Many vendors offer a partner locator tool on their website. This just lists the partners, and maybe gives you their certification level. It's certainly a step up from using the phone book or the web to find solution providers on your own.

No matter how you find your potential trusted partner, there are some very important considerations for determining if they are right for you. Here is a list of some of the key attributes to look for:

Integrator Size

The size of your company and the extent to which you use technology will determine the size of the integrator that you'll want to do business with. I'm surprised at the number of people who don't really get this. A mismatch here will result in disappointment. Remember, we are talking about a tight partnership here. There are very qualified integrators ranging in size from a single entrepreneur working out of his house, to several hundred engineers, available to your business in your area. If you are a very small company and you engage a firm that is too large, you'll be insignificant to their business. If you have hundreds of users, a really small integrator is not going to be able to keep up.

One of the problems faced by any integrator that starts small and grows is that the technicians who are out in the field doing installations are also called to do re-active support. It cost a lot to keep technicians in the office waiting for something to go wrong. It is only when there is enough business to warrant that the reactive technicians are busy pre-configuring and testing equipment for up-coming installations, when they are not reacting to problems, that an integrator can afford two sets of engineers. Ask the question if it is not obvious. I know of several integrators who are interested only in making tons of money. You can get away with it in this field. In that scenario there is typically an owner who hires a small staff. The staff struggles to do implementations and support simultaneously, or the organization outsources on-going support to a third party. If you are committed to UGN, that simply will not do. Even if they are less expensive, it will cost you far more when you have a problem than whatever the difference in cost is between them and a truly dedicated company. If you peel the onion just a bit, these things will be evident. For this very reason large firms doing major projects will often ask that the response to their request for proposal includes the names and credentials of the staff doing the work . Meet the staff face to face. I am not at all suggesting that only a company with enough staff to split the responsibilities is right for your firm. I know some very dedicated individuals who work either out of their home or in a small office with just a couple of people. They do a tremendous job supporting the small companies that trust them for their networks. For them it is a perfect fit. Those same firms cannot take on a client with 100 users, however, without adding staff and changing the way things are done.

You may catch a company in the transition phase from small to medium size. If that is the case and you know and trust the owners, you can go into the relationship with your eyes wide open, and make it work. Have this book in your hand and insist that they read it, so they at least know the standard you are holding them to. We had some very solid and very trusting customers that worked with us through our transition in the early days. The one thing they always knew is that I was accessible 24/7/365, and the buck stopped here. I went out more than once when a technician was not available, and so did my partner. Those were challenging times, but many of the relationships we built continue to this day. These are some of our biggest fans. You're a business leader. Part of what got you here is your instinct. Make sure you use it and trust it, but also monitor the situation closely.

Solid References

The age old game is to provide only the top clients as references. Take the time to dig a little. Every project has its mis-steps, this stuff is just too complicated for it not to. Get into the details. How did the integrator approach the solution, tactically or strategically? What problems came up and how were they handled? Did they tie up the inevitable loose ends? Were the technicians polite, knowledgeable, thorough, informative? Did they take the time to show your people how to get the most out of the solution? Do they offer ongoing support, custom tailored to the customer's needs? How accessible is the company's leadership? Tailor these questions to reflect the things you glean as most important from reading this book. Be suspicious if everything was always fine.

If the integrator really is a trusted partner to the references who provide a solid history, you should be able to have a very frank conversation with their client about the integrator's strengths and weaknesses. No one is perfect. The real test of their mettle is how they act when things don't go well. Get references from the manufacturer of the product(s) they are implementing. Keep in mind that these folks sometimes walk a fine line, and other times they play games. They may suggest a less competent integrator simply because that integrator tends to look out more for the manufacturer's best interests than those of the customer. Be sure to get both client and manufacturer references, and give them equal weight.

Certifications

Knowledge is demonstrated primarily by manufacturer certifications in the IT industry. The most famous of these are Cisco and Microsoft certifications. Most manufacturers certify the individual technicians, and some, like Cisco and Microsoft, also certify the integration company. When I said that the failure to admit that they don't know everything is a weakness of not just your own technicians but also a fault with some integrators, I specifically had in mind those integrators who try to provide every type of solution there is in technology, without the certified staff to actually be competent at it. They are out there. Check the certifications, and check the number of implementations they have done involving the solution(s) you need.

One very important capability that is an absolute must for any integrator is the basic skill of designing and supporting the core of your backbone network. This core is made up of devices that route information across your network and switch the paths of that information instantly to assure the highest performance of all the devices on your network. In keeping with our very simple naming convention, these devices are called routers. In fact at a 2007 gathering of 20 of the top regional integrators in the US, Howard Charney, a Senior Vice President at Cisco Systems (who is part of Cisco's "Office of the President") pointed out that it's dangerous to discount the importance of basic networking philosophies in the converged network infrastructure world. "Don't give up hard-won expertise you have gained in switching and routing," Charney warned. You would be wise to make sure that your trusted advisor is an absolute expert in these basic competencies regardless of whatever else they are going to do for you. If not, they should demonstrate a very solid partnership with a firm that is. This leads me to my next point:

Partnerships

If you are fortunate enough to find a trusted partner who is completely open and honest about what they cannot do, the very next question you want answered is how do they fill the holes? The best way is to have a strong on-going partnership with a company or companies that seamlessly fills those holes. It takes a wise businessman to know what his company doesn't know, and to be confidence enough in his own company's abilities to forge strong relationships with other companies, who can do what his company cannot. There should be a top level relationship between the senior leadership of both companies, and a demonstrated ability to work together for the good of their mutual clients. Once again, a few strong client references, investigated thoroughly, are essential.

Approach

By this I mean the approach of the salesperson who will handle your account. It is typical for the sales person to be very product focused, or solution focused. Such a sales person will spend most of his/her time telling you all about their company and all the great things they can do. That sounds OK, doesn't it? I would strongly suggest you interview several sales people until you find one or two who spend most of their time asking about your business. If they don't already have a relationship with you, you should expect questions about your industry, your philosophy, what is most important to you, what are your goals for your business, what technologies do you currently use in support of those goals, etc. There will be plenty of time later to discuss what technologies exist that you are not currently using that could help you further your business objectives. This first meeting will be focused on understanding your business if this integrator can truly be a trusted advisor.

Have you ever gone to a doctor with a problem and had that doctor quickly look at the problem and immediately suggest surgery? How comfortable were you? I can tell you I was quite uncomfortable. Even though the guy was a specialist, and I expected a level of confidence and competence, I expected a little more conversation. Contrast that to the doctor who asks a bit about you first. The conversation goes something like this: "Tell me a little more about how this condition might have developed? What was your normal routine in terms of diet, exercise, stress level, travel, etc? Did you change anything about that routine prior to the symptoms you are experiencing?"

There is a really good chance that the second doctor is going to give you several more treatment options, and will take a lot more interest in your long-term success, in treating the problem and in preventing a recurrence. It's a very similar approach that you want to see from the sales person of your trusted partner. One note of caution. If you have been doing business with a company for some time, but you have delegated that responsibility and not been actively involved, you may need to guide the conversation a bit by simply indicated to the salesperson that you are interested in taking the relationship to a different level. A sharp sales person will recognize the opportunity and have the kind of meeting I am suggesting. If not, keep looking.

You may be tempted, because you are in a high position, to bypass the salesperson and go right to the top of the integration firm. Resist the temptation. Start with the salesperson who will be your regular contact person. It is a good idea to ask that person to set up a meeting with the leaders of his/her company, after you have established that they are a potential trusted partner company. What happens far too often is that the leader of the company thinks at your level, but their sales people don't. That's a sign in and of itself of poor leadership, and you'll want to consider another firm. If you like the firm enough but don't particularly care for this one sales person, you may privately request that a different sales person be assigned to your account. You could be doing the potential partner a favor. They will gladly honor your request and either re-train the less strategic sales person or open up his/her employment options.

Project Management

Because of the complexities of technology, it is critical to manage the many resources that will have to come together to make the implementation go well. Mathew Schwartz, a freelance business and technology journalist based in Cambridge, MA, in a September 2007 article discussing success in technology projects had this to say; "Memo to senior managers: To maximize success rates, all projects need a project manager, or at least someone who plays one." Your trusted partner must have capable project managers. You need to ask some very direct questions about how they will handle your project.

Do they manage the entire project, including any other outside vendors that may be involved? What tools do they use to manage the project? What kind of verbal/written communication can you expect during the project? How do they track and tie up the loose ends from a project? Again, look for certifications. Project Management Professional (PMP) certification is a professional credential recognition managed by the Project Management Institute (PMI). PMP certification requires a high school degree, 7500 hours in a lead role, experience performing management tasks over a period of 60 months, and completion of 35 hours of project management learning within the past eight years. For critical projects insist that the project manager be certified.

Knowledge Transfer

Unlike the real estate or insurance agent in *Freakonomics*, a good trusted partner in the technology world is going to make the transfer of knowledge to your staff a vital part of the implementation and on-going support of your network. As soon as you have made the decision to invest in new technology that your staff has not implemented, it will be imperative that they gain the knowledge required to incorporate the on-going support of that technology into their daily routine. Depending on the technology, this can happen in several ways. They can either attend training prior to the implementation, during the implementation, or after the implementation. Your trusted advisor will work all three types of training into their strategy for transferring the knowledge that they have to your staff. The timetable for doing so will depend on your objective for supporting the technology for the entire time that that technology serves your business needs.

This is referred to as the *lifecycle* of the technology. Again it varies from company to company, based on how long the technology enables your company to thrive. An integration company should not just be OK with sharing their knowledge, but should actually make it a priority.

Some companies do function like those examples in *Freakonomics*, and you definitely want to avoid any company that hoards knowledge or is unwilling to openly share all that they know with your staff. The pace of change in technology ensures integrators have to work ourselves out of the business of supporting older technologies that are still valid in our client's networks, in favor of new leading edge technologies. We do so by transferring that support capability to our client's support staff. It doesn't mean that we don't play any role in the support of the older technologies; it just means that our client's staff has become so familiar with the technologies that they can directly support end users and do most of the troubleshooting and resolution of problems that occur. Our role then becomes minimal and may simply include monitoring for problems, and sparing replacement units as part of the problem resolution process. As with everything we've discussed, the situation varies from client to client, depending on the technology, staff, budget, etc. The bottom line is that your trusted partner should always be bringing you new technologies to advance your business, and enabling your staff to learn and assume support of those technologies as soon as is practical. The rapid pace of technology requires the advise, expertise, competence, experience, and transfer of knowledge that a trusted partner brings to the table.

On-going Support

When I say Utility Grade I am referring to continual daily performance, or the effectiveness of your IT. You have to know your network is performing to peak at all times. You also need to know that there are more technical eyes than yours watching the network and gathering all the detailed performance information that you don't need to know or understand. A trusted partner is going to have a fully staffed network operations center that monitors your network whenever you need it. For most companies that is 24/7/365. For some, it may begin an hour or two before, and end and hour or two after, normal working hours. Whatever your need may be, your partner must demonstrate extreme competence in this area. What happens when a fault condition occurs? You need to know how they handle problems. They should have a call ticket system that provides multiple call generation methods. If a fault occurs on the network, either the monitoring system itself or the person monitoring the system must generate an electronic call ticket.

You, or your staff depending on the severity of the ticket, should automatically be notified of a call ticket at its creation, and when it is closed. Keep in mind that a fault may not necessarily indicate that your users are experiencing downtime. The fault may be a threshold that has been exceeded that would indicate that a system might fail soon if preventative action was not taken. A fault may indicate that a primary system has switched to a backup system, again with no outage to the user, but that primary system should be fixed as soon as possible. The notification system that your partner uses must be flexible enough to be fully customized to your wants and needs. You decide, not based upon the technology itself but based on your business needs, just who gets notified when, and how often, until the problem is resolved. As I explore the idea of keeping your finger on the pulse I'll discuss the notifications that I believe are important to you specifically. It will be based on the number of users affected and the importance of the functions that they are temporarily either unable to perform or can't perform as effectively as they should.

I hope you can see how important it is that your trusted partner clearly understands your business. Every aspect of what they provide to your company must be clearly and effectively tied to your business objectives. Examine their ability to tailor the ongoing support they provide to your specific needs. This is a key differentiator between just another provider, and a trusted partner. Many Value Added resellers consider the value they add to be the mere fact that they have re-active support programs, or even pro-active monitoring. That is all well and good, but if it is cookie cutter and cannot be custom tailored to your specific needs, it has value - but not enough value. Make sure the whole package is there: proactive monitoring, reactive support, a dedicated team of competent problem resolution engineers, etc. Beyond that though, trust your gut as you ask the deeper questions about tailoring the service to your needs including the monitoring hours, reaction times, notification process. I believe it will become apparent just how good a fit the integrator is to your business.

With the right attitude, the right staff, and the right trusted partner Information Technology will truly become a strategic advantage for your company. It is not uncommon today, for the market value of a business to be affected by the IT infrastructure.

Chapter 6
Physical Environment

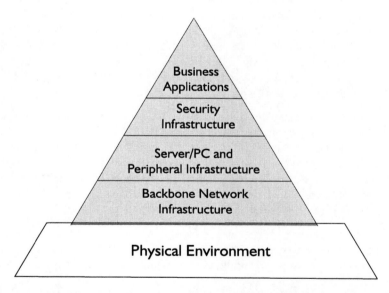

Business Applications

Security Infrastructure

Server/PC and Peripheral Infrastructure

Backbone Network Infrastructure

Physical Environment

There are some widely recognized best practices for what our industry calls the Network Critical Physical Infrastructure (NCPI), or the physical environment that is critical to your network. It is the bottom, fundamental building block of UGN's hierarchy of needs. As such, it is the foundation upon which the Information Technology (IT) and Telecommunication (Telecom) networks reside. It provides power, cooling, physical housing, physical security, fire protection, and cabling which allow the Information Technology to function.

Depending upon which of many studies regarding NCPI performance you reference, 40 to 60 percent of infrastructure downtime is associated with human error. This includes accidents, spills, incorrect cabling, programming mistakes, etc. It stands to reason then, that the other 40 to 60 percent of downtime results from equipment failure or network outages. The former have a lot to do with the right people as we discussed in Chapter 3. Even with the right people your policies and procedures are absolutely essential as are the proper level of accountability, particularly for those who have access to the core infrastructure with the highest potential for crippling the largest number of users – and therefore bleeding the most money. For the latter, it comes down to some key areas that comprise the NCPI and how well the critical infrastructure is designed, implemented, and supported.

The lifecycle of the physical infrastructure is typically 10 to 15 years. Think about that. How often do you invest in something that is going to last for 15 years? The implication is that the physical infrastructure will be in place for a number of turnovers in networking equipment. The average lifecycle of your network backbone infrastructure is four to five years. The physical infrastructure may even have to move to a different location with you.

So much can happen in technology and to your business during the lifecycle of your physical infrastructure that it is critical to plan for change in the initial investment. One very interesting statistic in larger organizations is that their data centers typically run at 30 to 50% of capacity. Five years is about as far as I can look forward and still have any confidence that my predictions will come true. I have a tendency to be more conservative, so my five year plans have typically been exceeded. It would appear from this statistic that larger firms have the opposite problem.

There is a standard for data center infrastructure established by the Telecommunication Industry Association and referred to as TIA-942, "Telecommunications Infrastructure Standard for Data Centers." This standard specifies the minimum requirements for both telecommunications and facilities infrastructures, and establishes a topology for connecting and accessing these elements. In addition, the standard recommends ways to achieve a manageable balance between architectural, mechanical, and electrical design considerations.

TIA-942 Annex G classifies data centers from Tier I to IV in terms of the site-level infrastructure required to sustain specific levels of uptime. This tier model has become standard language to connect uptime goals with the level of redundancy built into the data center infrastructure.

The tiers progress upward as single points of failure are eliminated. Tier I is a non-redundant system where a failed component is replaced while the system remains in a down state. Data centers achieving Tier II contain at least one set of fully redundant capacity components (i.e., N+1 capacity) such as uninterruptible power supply (UPS) units, and cooling and chiller units. Tier III data centers arrange redundant capacity into multiple distribution pathways, including power and cooling functions, and Tier IV systems extend fault tolerance to any and every system that supports IT operations.

All of this redundancy has a price, not just in terms of equipment costs, but also in the amount of space required to house the additional equipment. As single points of failure are eliminated, more facilities equipment is required to support redundant capacity and distribution. It also is important to note that the data center itself is rated only as high as the weakest subsystem that will impact site operations. It is highly unlikely that you will want to obtain a tier certification for your data center infrastructure unless you have a very large data center or are specifically delivering technology-based services to industries that require you to have such certifications. The point of bringing it to your attention is that the standards, if you choose to have your IT staff research them, give you a framework for establishing and obtaining specific performance goals.

It is also worth noting here that there is an organization called the Uptime Institute. As the name implies, they are dedicated to helping companies achieve maximum uptime for their IT networks. If you fish around their site you will find a Total Cost of Ownership calculator. It is designed for very large organizations and you may not be able to tailor it to your specific needs, but it is worth some time to study it so that you can shift your thinking from straight purchasing costs to all of the surrounding factors that impact the cost of running your network. I like to think black and white which can sometimes be detrimental when trying to think outside the box. Studying this tool in particular, and others like it, help to provide a broader perspective. Their website is www.uptimeinstitute.org.

You have NCPI in your company. It either just happened, or it was carefully planned. If it just happened chances are you chose a suitable room and equipped it with some sort of air conditioning, then placed equipment in the room either on tables or shelves of some sort. If you deemed the equipment critical enough you probably put some sort of power protection in place, and hooked it all up. I've seen a lot of closets and backrooms, even broom closets in which cleaning supplies co-exist with routers and switches. The war stories could fill volumes. In my own company we started with a single server sitting on a desk running an old Novel proprietary networking software system. We now have a robust, fully redundant, secure rack system with power and air conditioning, generator back up, etc. We grew into that. It didn't happen overnight. If you started small and have grown as a company but have not really addressed this issue, you should. If it was carefully planned you probably answered a) to question 3 of the test, and are just reading this to be sure you didn't miss anything. That's OK too. It never hurts to be doubly sure.

Proper investment in NCPI is for risk management. It's an insurance policy against network downtime. Your equipment can operate pretty well in even the worst of environments. It just cannot do so for as long or as reliably as it can operate in the best environment. The APC five nines number I referenced earlier was based on an NCPI that is designed, implemented, and supported at the highest levels – and highest cost – available. In TIA terms it would be considered a Tier IV certified data center. It is likely not fully practical or affordable for your network. There are some best practices, however, that provide a good balance between cost and risk. You should note that cost in that scenario refers not just to acquisition costs, but also to operational costs including ongoing service of the equipment. In other words the total cost of ownership (TCO) as identified in the TCO tool that The Uptime Institute offers. Risk as stated earlier, includes not just the risk of downtime, but also of obsolescence due to investment in systems that are outgrown before their lifecycle ends. Ideally you want to be investing in a system that can grow with your company, but for which that ability does not carry a huge price premium. You don't want to overspend to the point where your investments are severely underutilized, but you also don't want to underspend on a system that will have to be completely replaced as you expand. Modularity typically means agility. You pay a little more for a well designed modular system but adding to it as you grow is less expensive, and less disruptive (less planned downtime – which as you know from Chapter 1 does cost you money).

Another key issue is standardization. I believe strongly in standardizing on a particular manufacturer's product in each critical area of your network. This has a number of advantages. First it provides for predictable costs for the lifecycle of the technology as your network grows. Second it provides for more manageable training costs. Third it reduces overall maintenance costs (assuming it is not under-supported legacy equipment – which we'll discuss in Chapter 7), which include mean time to repair, sparing of critical systems, and redundancy costs. And finally, it provides a level of consistency in a constantly changing environment. Remember, unlike most areas of technology investment, the turnover of your NCPI is usually over ten years.

Let's take a look then, at some of the critical investment areas of your NCPI:

Power

The degree to which you protect not only the condition of power into your equipment but also the actual delivery of power will vary based upon your needs. In developing countries it is obvious that power generators are a basic requirement for any business. In developed countries however, the source of power is usually very consistent, as is the quality of the power. (Although the CEO of a bank in Maine rejected the premise of my argument that IT must function as any other utility – the power utility in his area is apparently often out!) IT equipment is quite sensitive to fluctuations in power and should be protected from spikes or degradations that could cause damage. Data loss should be mitigated as well by having a power back up scenario that at a minimum provides for an orderly shut-down of critical servers, in the event of a total power outage. An orderly shut-down assures that data is not corrupted, and that users can save critical data for work being performed at the time of the outage. Very few businesses can function without power, but some businesses absolutely must. For such businesses generator power must be supplied in the event of an extended power outage. It is best that the design include an automatic transfer switch to transfer between utility and generator power.

Protecting equipment from power fluctuations and facilitating orderly shutdown is typically accomplished by an Uninterruptible Power Supply (UPS). These vary in size and capacity from very small devices designed for a single computer or peripheral to very large fully redundant complex systems designed to serve entire data centers. In the case of generator back-up UPSs should be included to handle the output of the transfer switch, since power will fluctuate considerably during the transfer.

UPS designs can be as simple as a one for one capacity where the UPS is capable of supplying the exact amount of power needed for a set period of time, referred to simple as an "N" design, to a more complex implementation where the UPS system itself is fully redundant and capable of providing some level of power greater than its own input level, referred to "N + X" where "X" is a factor of 1 or more times greater capacity. A much more detailed explanation can be found at the website of the Uptime Institute, or in several white papers provided on line at the website of American Power Conversion, a premier provider of NCPI systems.

Cooling

Cooling can be as simple as a traditional air conditioner mounted in a window or through a hole in the wall or can be a complex system of water chillers and air handlers that are embedded in the overall HVAC system of a building. The first is usually found in very small companies while the second is found in very large computer rooms. There is a complete science to everything in between that is beyond the scope of this book. The most important consideration is that air must be constantly circulated and maintained at maximum operating efficiency for IT equipment of about 72 – 75 degrees Fahrenheit (22 -24 degrees Celsius). IT equipment operates best at 35 -50% relative humidity. Traditional comfort air conditions are optimized for operation for only 1200 hours a year and at 80 Degrees Fahrenheit (27 degrees Celsius) and 50 % relative humidity. Too much humidity induces corrosion in critical computer components, while too little humidity increases static electricity. Precision air systems are designed to run 24/7/365 and to maintain optimal temperature and humidity in all seasons. This is often overlooked, particularly in smaller companies, but it doesn't have to be. Even the smallest data center can use a stand up, self contained precision air system for not much more than a good wall mount air conditioner. The capacity of precision air systems is measured in kilo-watts versus the traditional British Thermal Units (BTUs) that you may be familiar with for describing the capacity of air conditioners. Most people think of air conditioning as a summer requirement only. This kind of thinking overlooks the fluctuations in temperature and humidity that take place on a continual basis in any environment. Such fluctuations are damaging to critical networking components. Think of UGN as Bubble Boy and you get the picture...

There is an organization in the US called the American Society of Heating, Refrigerating and Air-Conditioning Engineers (ASHRAE) that is dedicated to this topic. Their website is www.ashrae.org .

Racks and physical structure

99% of the electricity used by IT devices is converted into heat. Removing that heat from the device is done using a fan that circulates heat through the chassis of the device. The fan is mounted in different places depending on the device and how the device itself was designed to be mounted. Most IT devices are designed to be mounted in a rack that has an air circulation system working in conjunction with the device's internal air flow. If the device is not mounted into a rack with proper airflow, or if several devices are simply stacked up on a desk or table, the performance and the longevity of the device will be compromised. The degree to which it is compromised will depend on how much heat it generates, how many devices are stacked, and if there is any air flow around the device at all. I have seen servers stacked on book shelves or on racks directly in front of solid walls with little space for air flow. These devices worked somehow, but not well or for very long. This is ludicrous considering the fact that a simple stand up, two post open aluminum 19" or 23" IT rack, which consists of a pedestal and rails with threaded screw holes, costs less than a book shelf. It may not be ideal or esthetically pleasing, but it does the job. The next step up from that is a four post open rack for heavier equipment and beyond that is an enclosed rack system with front and rear locking doors that can be equipped with a fan. It's maybe three to four times the cost of a decent bookcase. In every case, a set of vertical and horizontal cable managers along with necessary patch panels for easy termination make the racks as neat as humanly possible. The top of the line is a rack enclosure that includes a rack-mounted UPS, cooling fans, and a complete wiring management system. These can be equipped with all kinds of nifty features including network management, security etc. It comes down to how critical the systems are to your operation and how much you are willing to spend to protect them.

There is no excuse, however, for not rack-mounting the equipment, and keeping it neat and orderly. You can even buy half racks, that are half the height but have all the features of a full rack. Equipment that is not designed to be mounted in a rack should be placed on shelves that can be mounted onto the most basic rack. A perforated shelf is preferable for air flow.

The room should be neat with the racks placed far enough from walls to allow easy access to the front and back of the racks. I am not suggesting that you need to invest in an expensive raised floor computer room. In fact, at least one school of thought is that raised floors are not only unnecessary, but provide less stability in the event of disasters such as earthquakes. The technology that makes raised floor unnecessary for most NCPI environments is the development of specialized racks and their associated cabling and cooling systems, along with cable trays and ladders that are easily installed above equipment racks. Regardless of how you decide to do it, every piece of equipment purchased for your network has to be properly mounted and maintained in the proper environment.

There is a nice white paper offered by a manufacturer of cabling systems called

Panduit, who wrote the paper in conjunction with other vendors Cisco and APC. It is called "Facility Considerations for the Data Center" and can be found at www. panduit.com .

Security

There are many aspects to security around IT which will be extensively discussed in a separate chapter specifically devoted to it. In regard to NCPI we'll focus on the physical security aspect of a complete Identity and Access Management (IAM) system. Most companies recognize the need to control physical access to critical networking equipment and systems. This can range from a simple locked door to a more complex access system that could require a special badge or a biometric reader. The most secure system I've encountered involved a glass booth that not only required biometrics, but also weighed each person on the way into the computer room and on the way out. I honestly thought that was overkill, but I was impressed by it. I've been to government facilities that didn't have anything near that kind of security.

At the root of security of your critical infrastructure is who can get to it, and what can they do once they get there. This may seem to be common sense, and it is. Yet, 60% of data center downtime is caused by human error. The more you are able to limit not just who can get physical access to the computer room, but also what they can do when they get there, the better chance you have of beating these statistics.

Your well defined physical security plan should provide at least three lines of defense. The first is who gets into your building and why. That is really at the heart of your total IAM system: who gets to what, why, and what do they actually do when they get there. In the case where your company is required to keep track of such things for regulation compliancy reasons, this is what an auditor will want to know. It should include not just your procedures but a valid historical record that demonstrates those procedures in action.

A well defined procedure for accepting and controlling guests is important. Once inside your building guests should require an escort to wherever it is they are going. If it is not practical that someone be with the guest every moment a second layer of defense is a locked door to the computer room. Only those requiring access should have it. Anyone else allowed in must be logged in by an escort who is with them at every moment. There is a third layer of defense. Individual racks can be locked if they contain extremely critical devices that only a very small subset of users are ever required to access. In this way you control not only who can get in, but what they can do as well. The human error percentage is quite high in this area. It makes sense that if you keep critical equipment separated by functional areas into individual locking cabinets, this danger is reduced.

As we will discuss later, the biggest threat to most of the devices in your network is not necessarily physical in nature. Still, a well defined and tightly enforced physical security plan that is part of your overall IAM policy is absolutely essential.

Fire protection

Historically, fires have had a significant negative impact on business. Industry studies cited by the Fire Suppression Systems Association show that 43 percent of businesses closed by a significant fire never reopen, and another 29 percent fail within three years.

Fire detection and protection for data centers has progressed extensively in recent years. The smoke detector remains the most effective means of detection and there are a variety of smoke detectors ranging from very simple and inexpensive to very complex and expensive. The proper device depends on the size and scope of your installation. Once a fire is detected having the proper system in place to quickly extinguish the fire is critical. Most electrical fires are identified as Class C fires. A simple Class C fire extinguisher for a small computer room would suffice. A larger room will require a fire suppression system. The Fire Suppression Systems Association is a trade group dedicated to the proliferation of proper fire suppression systems for all types of businesses. They describe fire protection tools that protect highly valuable and sensitive areas, Clean Agent Fire Suppression Systems. Clean agent systems not only protect your data center as well as its contents from fire damage, but are safe for your people as well.

Clean agent systems can react quickly to extinguish a fire at its earliest stages. Using early detection and rapid extinguishment, clean agent systems eliminate the fire, reduce the damage to equipment, and increase the safety of people in the fire area. Clean agents extinguish fires as a gas, which gives them the ability to penetrate into cabinets and obstructed areas. It also makes them uniquely suited to protect the electronics hidden inside a piece of equipment, a likely place for a fire to start. By thoroughly flooding the area with a gaseous fire fighting agent, even obscured or hard to reach fires are quickly extinguished, often long before they can be seen. After extinguishing, the agent is readily ventilated from the room along with any byproducts of the fire.

The agents are non-conductive and non-corrosive, making them safe to use on and around live electrical equipment. There is no residue to cleanup, no lingering materials to slowly degrade equipment, and no need for an expensive "Disaster Recovery" process. Operations are brought back online and productive in a very short time.

Most agents are also safe to use in occupied areas. These agents have undergone extensive toxicity testing to prove they are compatible with people. While the National Fire Protection Association recommends exiting the hazard in the event of a fire, it is important that people not be harmed by the extinguishing system.

In today's world of increasing global competition, simple fire protection may not be enough. Equipment downtime and loss of records, archival storage, and ultimately ongoing operations could have a severe effect on your operation and possibly that of your customers.

Cabling

No matter the size of your data center, there is a complex cabling scheme lurking there. Walk into any computer room, ours included and you will immediately see what I mean. The interconnection of different devices, with various types of cables and connectors, in a constantly changing environment makes management of cabling one of the most difficult and frustrating parts of IT. I've personally wired new equipment into environments, painstakingly cutting and crimping to optimal length, then carefully routed and labeled each cable, only to come back to the customer site just a few weeks later and find a rat's nest. This makes a documented cabling strategy absolutely essential, for even with a carefully documented and enforced strategy, keeping it under control is extremely challenging.

A significant portion of TIA-942 identifies the many types of cables and the locations of equipment and how they recommend that all of these be inter-connected.

To discuss this properly we have to look at physical locations of various types of equipment and wiring. The first is the entrance room, or where circuits from outside vendors come into your building. These include your phone lines, Internet access, etc. Somewhere in that room is a sizeable piece of plywood onto which the circuits are terminated. This is called the demarcation (demarc) point. It is owned by the provider and you are allowed to wire from that point to your own data center, or computer room as you may refer to it. TIA-942 refers to the point where you bring wiring from the demarc to your own cabling infrastructure connected to your backbone equipment as the Main Distribution Area (MDA) In many smaller companies, the entrance room and computer room are one and the same. The standard does address this and recognizes that every company will have a different physical topology. Many companies I've been to simply started putting computer equipment in the same room where they had their phone system years ago, and that became the computer room by default.

Cabling is and always has been a complex issue. With constant advances in technology come constant advances and changes in the types of connectors used in the design of the equipment. The design of the cables themselves changes as well, though a bit less frequently. Standards for the types of sheathing on cables used have changed as fire codes have tightened. Most of this cabling involves very thin wires twisted together very precisely in order to carry data at high speeds. The higher the speeds the more strictly the twists per inch must be controlled, due to the electrical characteristics of the signals passing through them. It is quite mind boggling to consider that millions of minute electronic impulses are passing through these tiny wires each second.

Significant changes in fiber optic laser technology have occurred in recent years and more and more fiber optic cabling is being used for increased data speeds as well. Proper handling of fiber optic cables is extremely important. Stretching a fiber optic cable, for example by pulling it tightly around a corner, can damage the fibers and cause data loss. There are specific cable management devices that can be installed where you are routing fiber cables to help control the bend radius, which assures optimal performance.

A little education for your staff here goes a long way, but is extremely rare. Most people assume that if you work in IT you know all about the interconnecting cables and connectors. The truth is that new connectors and cable just seem to show up on a regular basis as technology advances, and as an IT person you are just expected to know, while there is very little training on the subject. This has been a source of frustration for as long as I've been in this business. There is an organization called BICSI that provides for vendor neutral certification training that is recognized around the globe. Visit www.bicsi.org for more information.

Ongoing Service and Support

For all elements of your network, a comprehensive management and on-going support plan is essential to preventing un-planned downtime. This is critical for your NCPI. As we'll discuss in detail on Chapter 10 the need to know about potential problems before they affect end users is crucial to preventing the productivity losses discussed in Chapter 1. You need to make the shift from reactive, where Mean Time to Repair is at a maximum (this is the time where you are bleeding profusely!) to a proactive approach that minimizes or even eliminates downtime. You have to make some key decisions that have an impact on the potential losses you face. It's your responsibility to make the decisions, and your IT staff's responsibility to adhere to them. First, will you have redundancy built in to your power, and to what level? The highest level is a redundant source of power using a generator. If not, will you at least have a battery back -up system? If so, how long will it provide power? Long enough for people to continue to work for an hour or two, or just long enough for an orderly shutdown of your critical systems to prevent data loss? If you have powered racks, will there be redundant power supplies in the individual racks? If not, how will you spare additional power supplies in case of an outage?

It is not enough to just put the stuff in place. It must be tested on a regular basis, and the results have to be well documented. It must be serviced on a regular basis as well. You don't want to discover that your back-up generator won't start the one time this year that you lose facility power.

Finally, your systems need to be SNMP compatible. The Simple Network Management Protocol (SNMP) is a set of rules that govern how a piece of equipment will communicate with a network management software system in order to determine the status of the device at any moment. It is the network management software that will then report that status to you or your staff via a visual display, or some type of alert message sent through e-mail, pager, etc. Every device you put on your network that is of any consequence to your daily operation needs to support this protocol, and needs to be monitored at all times that your business needs the device in order to function at peak efficiency. An alarm condition such a device needs to set in motion a response that recovers from the alarm state in the shortest possible time. If you have full redundancy your staff can respond when it is most convenient for them. You are not bleeding money because the redundant system is doing the job. Short of full redundancy a clear set of reaction times and escalation procedures must be pre-defined and tightly enforced to minimize UGN's bleedings. This brings a whole set of decisions regarding reactive support that are also addressed in Chapter 10.

Your response to UGN's need for a solid foundational physical environment will determine how well he is able to perform at all higher levels. This includes the backbone infrastructure level to which we will now turn our attention.

Summary

UGN, like you or I, cannot be healthy in an unhealthy environment. We've summarized the critical strategies, and the key areas of investment below.

Critical Strategies

◆ Understand the unique environmental requirements of IT equipment
◆ Protect your investments
◆ Plan for orderly shut down
◆ Test all systems regularly
◆ Monitor critical systems continuously

Written Plans

◆ Physical security plan
◆ Orderly shut-down procedures
◆ Detailed floor plan
◆ Detailed cabling plan

Key Investments

◆ Power condition, backup
◆ Racks

◆ Adequate HVAC
◆ Cabling management
◆ Fire protection
◆ Managed devices

Chapter 7
Backbone Network Infrastructure

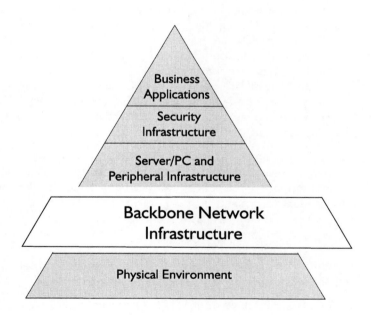

We need to recapitulate a few points made earlier, as we move to the second layer in UGN's hierarchy of needs. First the simplicity of our networking terminology is superficial, since it will help to introduce a few important terms. Second is the need to invest wisely. Investing wisely means assuring optimal performance for your investment dollar. Everything we discuss in this chapter carries that as its basic objective. Third is the lifecycle concept. The lifecycle for any technology you invest in will be the amount of time that the technology is useful to support your business objectives. During the entire lifecycle the technology must be constantly evaluated and maintained to peak performance, and it must be protected. Which leads to our final introductory point: you must *know* that it is performing well and is safe at all times.

UGN's backbone is just as the name implies – the backbone of your network upon which everything else depends. It is where we take the discussion up a level from the environment that forms the foundation of UGN's hierarchy of needs, to the point where some actual constructive flow of information is able to take place. I need to address an area that is widely propagated throughout our industry, but so misunderstood that it has cost companies incredible amounts of money. Many books have been written about it, and it has been touted as the miracle cure for IT woes. It is the concept of alignment, most often described as aligning your business objectives with your technology investments. It is a very noble idea, and it can work extremely well. But let's take a look at how it has fared in practical application. The consulting firm of Bain & Company found that companies grew faster and lowered costs more dramatically by first focusing on making their IT departments effective. Those that favored alignment before effectiveness, on the other hand, faced tougher growth prospects and higher spending rates. The objective of this book is to help you make your IT more effective. If you try to do alignment on a network that is ineffective, you will waste a lot of money and get extremely frustrated. In fact, Bain polled technology and business executives at 450 publicly-traded companies, asking two questions. First how is IT aligned with the business organization? Secondly how effective – getting projects done as specified, on budget and on schedule – those IT departments have been. 85 percent of respondents characterized their IT operations as ineffective. Did you catch that?? 85 percent!

Don't get me wrong. I am not suggesting alignment is a bad thing. I am telling you it is only a good thing if you first implement the suggestions in this book in order to make your Information Technology more effective. Of the firms Bain polled, those achieving effectiveness and alignment saw their three-year compound annual growth rate jump 37 percent, while IT spending rates dropped by more than ten percent. Now get this; companies that achieved effectiveness but not alignment cut IT spending by more than 17 percent and boosted growth by more than ten percent. In either of these last two cases the facts speak for themselves. If you do it right (effectively), IT actually costs you less in the long term.

The single most important need that UGN has is the need for a strong and effective backbone infrastructure.

In case you are not familiar with them, I'll review some basic backbone infrastructure terms. I mentioned the Internet Protocol (IP) as the way that your network devices take useful data and package it for travel throughout your network and, in the case of the Internet for example, perhaps throughout the world. As soon as you connect your computer to any other networking device, they will communicate with each other using IP. When you connect a number of devices together, they need a device that will control the flow of information between the two devices. This device is called a switch, because it switches information between the connected devices.

When you connect a number of computers and peripheral devices to the switch you have created a network. If the network is confined to a limited space, which could also be called the local area, you've created a Local Area Network (LAN). When you want to send information beyond your local area, you need a device that will route your information to another local area, and that device is referred to as a router. When the router sends information outside of your local area, either via an Internet connection or a direct circuit between two locations, it is said to be sending traffic to the wide area, thus forming a Wide Area Network (WAN). You probably already have a router in your home that connects you to the Internet. If you installed it yourself you likely connected your Internet service to the WAN port of the router and connected your computer to the routers LAN port. Congratulations, you are a networking expert. Well, sort of...

The router in your home that connects you to the Internet is a very basic router. It was not likely very expensive, but it does a lot. It is actually a combined router and switch in one device, which is why it likely has several LAN connections on the back. It probably also includes some basic security features, so it also functions as a basic firewall against outside threats to your home computer. In many cases the home router even includes wireless connection capability. No matter what is included in your home device it is intended to be just that, a device for the home. It is not intended to, and will do a poor job of, performing in all but the very smallest of business environments. It helps that you have it though, to help you understand what constitutes the backbone infrastructure of the business network. Each one of the devices we have talked about; the switch, the router, the wireless router, and the firewall, are all combined in some number depending on the size of your company, to form your network.

With regard to the IP language that these devices speak, it is important to understand a little about how each IP device is uniquely identified. Each device that connects to a network must specifically ask for a unique identifier, which is an IP address. If you configured your home router you may recall that it asked in the setup process, if your Internet provider was going to automatically give you an IP address for the device when it was connected to your Internet modem via the WAN port. (I apologize if you never have hooked up a home router, but you'll still be able to follow the explanation.) In most cases the answer to that question is yes. The process is referred to as dynamic addressing, because the device requests and receives the address only when it needs to connect to the network. The device that gives out addresses runs a process called dynamic host (individual devices on a network are referred to as hosts on a deeper technical level) configuration, by running software called the Dynamic Host Configuration Protocol (DHCP). Just about every network has a DHCP server. Here is where it gets pretty interesting, and challenging. There are public addresses that are available on the Internet and are tightly controlled and in limited supply. No device can get on the Internet without one of these public addresses. You get them through your Internet Service Provider generally. Since there are not nearly enough of these addresses available for every computer on every private network in the world, and for security reasons which we'll discuss

77

later, you run a private addressing scheme using your own internal DHCP server on your internal network.

One last point and we'll move away from the technical details. While individual users' computers don't need an address when not on a network, and may be constantly on the move, as in the case of a laptop, it really doesn't make much difference how or where they get an address, or what address they get. The network is smart enough to track their address on the fly and make sure they get the information they need. All it takes is a valid address on the most basic level. Network resources, like web servers though, get a permanent address. It is called a static as opposed to a dynamic address. When you type the name of a server into your web browser (like www.google.com) the browser has to figure out the IP address of that server. It does so using another process called Domain Name Service. There are a number of DNS servers on the Internet that the browser can interrogate to find out the IP address, on the fly or in a regularly updated table stored locally, for any web server. If you type the name wrong and get that familiar message that the "website could not be found", it is because your browser asked a DNS server, and the DNS server had no record for that name and therefore could not return a valid address for the server. I said all that so you would realize that all traffic on all IP networks depends on correct IP addresses.

When you work on your own network with a private address, and then go out to the Internet, another process kicks in that runs on your firewall or your router, which translates your internal private IP address to an external public IP address. This process is known as Network Address Translation (NAT). Everything that happens either on public or private networks is recorded. Every time a computer accesses a resource it leaves a trail in a log file on a router, switch, firewall or some other type of networking device. It is possible therefore, to watch this stuff in real time. It is also possible to set up rules to control all of this activity. When we talk about protecting your network from outside attacks in Chapter 9, we will discuss how you can prevent the wrong people from doing harmful things to your network by watching where they are going and what they are doing, and automatically stopping them from doing things that are known to be harmful. I once got a behind the scenes look at a real case of Internet fraud. The investigator was able to subpoena records from Internet service providers, libraries, credit card companies, etc. to track down and confront a perpetrator. It was fascinating to see the level of detailed information available, and the cyber-forensics process that is now a normal part of law enforcement. You don't want to have to do after the fact forensics. Instead you need to invest wisely in equipment that has the ability to be constantly on the lookout for intruders and to stop them before they do any damage to, or steal any information from, your network.

It is not unusual for large organizations to have an entire team of people who focus on the whole issue of IP addressing. It is a vital part of the health of any network. Mis-configurations can bring a network, a resource, or a set of resources down hard. Finding the error can be extremely time consuming. It takes a high level of knowledge to map out an IP addressing scheme that assures maximum and robust legitimate access for authorized users while at the same time affords maximum protection for your network. Just looking at the various processes we've discussed, which are strongly over simplified, you can see that going in and out of your network, obtaining the proper type of address, and gaining access to all the resources that you need involves a well thought out and pre-configured plan. Once a high level resource maps out the plan, the actual process of implementing and maintaining it is rather monotonous. For that reason, this is an area where errors occur on a fairly regular basis. The overarching term used to describe these systems and their collective functions is referred to as Internet Protocol Address Management (IPAM). IPAM is accomplished in three ways: setting up the various systems described above individually, using a single appliance to perform all of these functions, or contracting a partner who offers IPAM services. In the latter case the partner will need to set some of these services up in your data center and manage them remotely.

You don't need to know much beyond this simple terminology. The people who design the networks, configure these devices, and keep them secure and performing at peak efficiency need to know a whole lot more. It gets incredibly complex, and the terminology stops being intuitively obvious. I'll give you a couple of examples before we put terminology aside – both involve a "virtual" network. If you are operating a network that includes multiple LANs connected together via some type of WAN, you may want to ensure that only certain users on that network get to some specific applications running on specific servers. One obvious example is your financial servers. If you only want accounting folks to access your accounting program on a specific server, you don't need to build a separate physical network to assure others cannot access that server. You can, in routers and switches that have this advanced security feature, configure a virtual connection between each of the accounting folks and the accounting server. The devices on each end encrypt the data and assure that it traverses the network directly between the two end devices without being intercepted or observed by any other device. For practical purposes it appears as a direct connection between the two devices, even though the devices are physically connected to networks with all kinds of other devices. One obvious reason for doing so would be if you have accounting people at multiple remote locations. Each one appears to have a direct connection to the accounting server. The set up of these secure connections to the exclusion of anyone other than those specific accounting people is thus referred to as a virtual local area network or VLAN.

If the WAN that you send data over consists of dedicated circuits that only your company uses, say between its locations, it is referred to as a private network. If however, you utilized the Internet or the public telephone network to connect your locations it is referred to as a public network. Any time your information travels across a public network it is vulnerable to interception and must be protected. That is typically done by encrypting the data between two points with additional hardware or software. Your data is then said to be traveling on a virtual private network or

VPN. In both cases encryption of the data assures that only those authorized to view and use the data are allowed to do so.

Now you know a lot more than your neighbor about networking. You are slowly approaching expert status. You won't truly be there until you can configure a virtual network across multiple devices on a network. That will take a lot of study. And will be a colossal waste of time for you as the owner/senior manager. These examples do start to give you an idea of how the whole concept of networking can quickly get extremely complex. Setting everything up right is crucial to the daily performance of every one of the people who rely on your network to get their jobs done. You don't need to know how it works. You do have to take responsibility for it, and that means at least understanding enough to make informed decisions that assure your network is as effective as it can be.

Critical decisions regarding your backbone network

Equipment Vendor

Pick a single vendor. According to a study by Sage Research, organizations with one networking vendor experienced a cost of ownership per endpoint 29 percent lower than that of a multi-vendor network. Standardization is key as I said in Chapter 2. One vendor's product will be best for your network based on a cost/feature analysis. Your IT staff, working with your trusted partner, can determine which one. Insist that for your backbone network it is only one. Stay away from what are called "point products" that perform a single function, unless your staff and partner are convinced that your needs absolutely require it. Even if the primary manufacturer offers a solution with a few less features, unless there is a feature missing that you absolutely cannot do without, give a little if it provides a common configuration interface, management, and support strategy. I say this as the founder of a company that has built its reputation on providing best of breed products for our clients. We do so only when there is a far superior product, or the solution required is not available from our major supplier. We don't want the added training, support, and relationship management expense any more than you do.

Network Design

There are countless ways to design a network. I have never encountered two networks exactly alike. I have encountered networks that are equally robust however, despite their design differences. There is a combination of science and art to this, and it requires truly brilliant minds. A seasoned network engineer can spot a shoddy design in a second, and poke holes in is. Some hackers are seasoned engineers. The design has to take many factors into account. What we look to avoid are single points of failure that will affect large percentages of users on a network. I say percentages instead of numbers of users because if you are a ten user company and five are affected by an outage you've lost 50 percent of your productivity. We will talk about redundancy in a minute, but you have to understand that there are advanced features in the more sophisticated manufacturers' products that help to make your network more robust.

What we look to do is make the network as robust as possible given the business objectives and budget. Some advanced features cost money, but they usually save more than they cost. Sometimes the savings can't easily be identified. Routers that are able to prioritize the flow of data based on how critical the application is to your business, for example, can increase your staff's productivity but it is difficult to quantify the results. If your IT staff want to purchase a router with advanced features to increase productivity you should take a good look at it. Remember that the total cost of ownership (what Gartner Group, a major IT research firm, coined as "TCO" back in the 80s) is largely comprised of the implementation and on-going support of the product. It will cost you about the same amount to implement and support the product that doesn't have advanced features, and you won't get the productivity gains, no matter what they are. Here is where you get into a major quandary if you are not standardized on a single vendor. Some of the most advanced features have not become industry standards yet, so if you have multiple vendors' products forming your backbone, you'll have to revert to the least common feature set.

Of course, you can overspend by buying products, even from your single vendor, with advanced feature sets that are not used depending on where these devices are in your network. This is where the art part of the art and science of network design comes into play. A trusted partner is going to sell you only what you need. A solution provider who is not really trustworthy is going to oversell when they can get away with it. We see it all the time. Vendor sales people are notorious for this. If you are making a major infrastructure purchase decision – and you get to define major – ask the tough questions. What am I paying for and what will it do for my network, at every point? Again, a trusted partner will take the time to explain it all in terms that make sense to you. If they go off on technical tangents don't be afraid to reel them in. Some of my favorite encounters have been with business owners who did not want to understand the bits and bytes, but wanted a thorough explanation in laymen's terms of what features they were getting and why. My favorite example was when the CEO of a hospital in Ghana flew to our headquarters for a marathon session on a core infrastructure design. We spent hours going over the design until he understood the features from the standpoint of what they were going to mean to the everyday performance of his network.

Growth has got to be factored in. Unlike the physical infrastructure, the lifecycle of the backbone infrastructure is only about three to five years. That is still a significant amount of time in the life of many small to medium businesses. You need to align your three to five year business growth projections with your network design. If you design to significantly less growth than you actually experience, it can require a complete swap out of your infrastructure (what we call a fork-lift upgrade) before it has served its full potential lifecycle. This will always cost you more than it should have. If you anticipate rapid growth, look for modular designs that cost a bit more up front but less as you grow and add modules to the existing chassis. If you overdesign, which as we pointed out earlier is the case of most large company data centers, you obviously spend more than you have to. Involve your technology council and get some solid growth predictions as your network is designed.

Level of Redundancy

As with your physical infrastructure, you need to decide what will happen when there is a failure in a device on your backbone. I am not just referring to a failure of the entire device. It is possible to design your equipment solution to have redundant parts within each device, such as a failover power supply or a failover central processor, even one for one, or one for "N" redundancy, where N represents switching or routing cards that support multiple users or networks. This comes with a cost. That inexpensive home router/switch/firewall includes no redundancy at all and all your users go down if any function fails. You don't want your business in that vulnerable a position. But you may not want to spend what it takes to have complete redundancy in every – or in any device.

I apologize in advance, but there is some additional terminology you need to be familiar with in order for this discussion to be useful. The first terms are "core" and "edge". I refer to the backbone as all the devices comprising your network's infrastructure, whether at the core or at the edge. A purist might argue the point, but I really don't care. For the purposes of this book and your managerial view of IT you may consider all the networking devices as forming the backbone infrastructure. Some will be located in your data center or computer room, or that little closet you are now going to upgrade based on the last chapter. Some of those devices will be switches that connect directly to your servers/storage device, and to the router(s) that connect(s) your LAN to the WAN. These devices form the core of your backbone infrastructure. You may, depending upon the number of employees in your company and the size of the building(s) you occupy, have several switches scattered around your building or your campus. These form the edge of your backbone infrastructure. Core devices are most critical because multiple edge devices connect to them, and the servers running the critical applications your users need to access connect to them as well. If a core device is down hard and there is no redundant device to perform its function, many users are idle and you are bleeding money at an extraordinary rate. Edge devices by design serve a smaller subset of users, so if one is down it only affects those particular users, so the bleeding is not as bad. It makes sense, based on that information, to have a much more robust redundancy and sparing strategy at the core, and to have more stringent protection and access rules for core devices than for edge devices.

The most important thing is that you make a conscious, informed decision as to what level of redundancy is practical and affordable for your network. Ask your IT staff/person what level of redundancy is in their network design, where, and why. If you have a lot of users, or multiple locations, the level of redundancy will vary based on the number of users who will be affected if the device were to fail.

Redundancy is not limited to equipment. Redundancy can also be included in the wiring between critical devices, the circuits between locations, or from your location to the Internet, and even the path that your information takes once in the WAN. All need to be considered. The average high speed (T-1) circuit is down for 8 hours per year. In the case of wiring, for example, if we are wiring from a critical switch in a data center to another switch on a separate floor where there are a large number of users, we will typically design redundant interfaces on the switched and redundant wiring between the two floors so that if either an interface falls or a cable is cut or broken all those users still function like nothing happened. You don't need to understand how the switch handles the incident or knows how to re-direct the traffic, but just understand on a practical level, what will happen when a device goes down. How will it affect your business? Think about the cost of just one outage – if it affects a number of users – when your IT folks ask you for enough budget money to implement a redundant design for your critical routers, switches, firewall(s), etc. It is all about risk, and it is a delicate balance.

Security

In every area of your network, security has to be built in to your design in such a way that it can be regularly monitored, tested, managed, and reported. We'll get deeper into those issues in Chapters 10 and 11. As we discussed in the last chapter you first have to consider the physical security of your backbone router, switches, firewall, and any other critical devices. These can be configured from any area of the network if you know the IP address of the device and can log in. That information must be closely guarded. As IT people leave your organization and they will, you need to make sure that passwords get changed on systems and equipment that they had access to. This is often overlooked or done haphazardly. We will discuss configuration management in a moment. Improperly configured devices can leave vulnerabilities at critical entry points into your network. The router(s) connecting your network to the Internet in particular must be securely locked down with no logical holes. It sounds simple, but it is not at all. When technicians work on devices or add various types of access that your users require, they have to create logical openings into your network. These must allow only your authorized users in, and keep everyone else out. The configuration to make this happen is very precise, detailed, and complex especially if there are a lot of access points in. You have to have regular vulnerability scans on your network for this reason. These are usually done by a third party.

Spare Parts

It is highly unlikely that you will have complete redundancy in every device in your network. More likely, you will have high levels of redundancy at the very core where most users would be affected by a failure, and little or no redundancy on the edges of your network where fewer users would be affected by a single device failure. In either case, in the event of a failure you will want to replace the failed device as soon as practicable. Where is the spare? It depends on a few factors. How critical are those users who are affected? In other words, how much money are you bleeding out while those users are rendered ineffective, yet are still on your clock? If the losses have the potential to be significant, but not so much so that you are willing to invest in full redundancy, you may instead invest in having a spare or spares at your location. In that case you decide on a 1 for "N" physical sparing strategy, where again "N" represents the ratio of devices per single spare unit. This helps to illustrate the importance of standardization I keep touting. Standardization not only reduces the amount of training your IT folks need, but also simplifies your sparing strategy. It may not prove cost effective for you to keep spares at your location at all. If you can tolerate a few hours of downtime, you may rely on your trusted partner company to stock spares for you. In that case you purchase a contract to that effect, with a specified response time during which a technician needs to arrive with a pre-configured spare to replace the failed unit. This leads me to the next very critical issue.

Configuration Archiving

If you have installed a home router more than a year or two ago, you had to put some configuration parameters in yourself. These days most home networking devices configure themselves. In a business network you will have a more complex configuration. Despite the best efforts, and great claims of many equipment vendors, this equipment doesn't configure itself. If a device does fail, or if it somehow should lose its configuration, it is critical that you have an electronic copy of that configuration stored somewhere. A lot of unnecessary downtime occurs for lack of a solid configuration archiving strategy, referred to as a Configuration Management Database (CMDB). Without a solid strategy for not just storing the initial configuration of each device, but also keeping the archived configurations updated any time a change is made to the network, you will lose additional precious time while a spare device is configured to replace a failed device. The most tragic thing I've observed in this regard is a spare being incorrectly configured either because of bad documentation or poor archiving practices, which actually then creates more problems when the incorrectly configured device is plugged in. It takes precious time, while your company bleeds money, to figure out that the new device, though working properly, is missing some critical configuration information that prevents it from correctly delivering information across the network. The pressure on the technician installing the device at that moment is intense. You should do everything possible to assure this never occurs.

The configurations of networking devices, reflecting the complexity of the network, are incredibly complex lines of code with very stringent syntax. Minor mistakes or variations can be extremely costly, as they can cripple a network and can be difficult to find and correct. Operator error is actually the leading cause of unplanned downtime. If you are trusting a partner for support of your network that includes a reactive element with spares in hand, you must be certain that there is a cooperative effort and consistent strategy that is strictly adhered to by both your staff and your partner's staff for configuration archiving. It is crucial for the mean time to repair, which is required to stop the bleeding from a device failure.

Change Management

Regardless of the size or complexity of your network, it is important to have a very precise process to control who is allowed to make changes to your backbone infrastructure and when. Remember that planned downtime is the only acceptable form of downtime. Changes should be well thought out and designed into the existing network well in advance of being implemented. Each time your IT folks plan to make changes of any significance to the backbone that require a configuration change, a precise plan must be put together that includes every line of configuration that must be changed/added/deleted. More than one person should review the proposed changes. The plan should include the chronological order in which every device that must be reconfigured to accommodate the proposed change is re-configured. In studying the impact of the change and constructing the change plan, they must be sure that the network documentation is current and reflects the actual configuration as it is now running in each device. They must also be sure that the plan includes updating the documentation after the change is implemented. Both your IT staff and your partner's staff should be required to sign off on the proposed change plan.

The execution of the plan should be scheduled at a time when the least number of users will be impacted. The scheduled time should be well communicated to the user community in advance. The plan must include a back-out strategy should the execution not go well, or not produce the desired results. Networks change constantly. If change is not properly managed, it will quickly get out of control, documentation will become outdated, and at that point your backbone network is a disaster in the making. One day it will come crashing down and UGN will bleed profusely. Under those circumstances it is not a question of if, it is a question of when.

Some of the above referenced changes will be the result of required maintenance. No vendor's operating code is flawless. Patches and fixes along with new features are made available on a regular basis. They often require an upgrade to the code in your backbone networking devices. Not every new release of code will apply to your network. It takes constant research on the part of your IT staff and partner to review vendor information on flaws and vulnerabilities. Whether a new release is applicable to the devices on your network may depend upon how your network is configured. If the new code does apply and must be applied to your devices it should be treated as outlined above, like any other change to your network.

Additions, moves, and changes for individual users that don't require major reconfiguration of devices obviously don't require a change plan. However they do require very specific procedures that include constant update to what must be extremely accurate documentation. Those are the daily details that your IT staff has to manage along with all this other stuff.

Monitoring and Maintenance

We devote an entire chapter (Chapter 10) to monitoring so we won't go into a lot of detail here. All backbone infrastructure devices **must** be monitored. I did not say should, I said must. It is not optional. There are a number of ways to do this ranging from free shareware to sophisticated systems with real-time portals/dashboard, etc. that allow constant monitoring of every critical device. As we discussed in Chapter 2, the best scenario is a proactive monitoring system that is able to detect the potential for failure and alert your staff to take corrective action to prevent it.

If you have built redundancy into the solution, it should be routinely tested for obvious reasons. It seldom is in my experience. Some vendors, like Cisco for example, have operating systems in their devices that perform "self-healing". This is one of the aforementioned advanced features and refers to the ability of some devices to provide alternate paths for the IP packets in the event of failure in the primary path. If that occurs, your staff should know and should restore the primary path as soon as possible. The good news in this scenario is that you are not bleeding money while they do so. I believe that you should be in the notification loop regardless of how senior your position in the company. This of course, depends on the size of the company and your management strategy. I hope you recognize the incredible costs of downtime and want to know immediately when you are bleeding money at all but the most trivial levels.

Which brings me to maintenance; your car needs routine maintenance. Nothing is routine about the maintenance of your backbone network. Anytime anyone touches it, it can be service affecting. We've already talked about how you should treat patches and fixes, additions or deletions, etc. Let's look at unplanned maintenance or reactive maintenance that occurs when something fails. The monitoring systems detect a problem or potential problem. A trouble ticket should be automatically generated that requires immediate acknowledgement. It is prioritized based on the criticality of the fault and the number of users affected. It includes specific notification processes, and has an automatic escalation process that tracks the length of time the ticket is open and escalates the ticket if it is not resolved within pre-determined time frames based upon its priority. A number of these trouble ticket systems exist, and most are available as a feature of the monitoring system or will interface directly into a monitoring system.

Regardless of how the trouble ticket is generated, someone, either your IT staff or your trusted partners staff, will need to react to it. In the best scenario, it is a tightly woven, cooperative effort between the two. This all depends on the staff you have and their level of competence. If you have a limited, but highly competent staff, they have better things to do than see every ticket and react to it. The first level of reactive support needs to be some basic investigation to determine the severity and complexity of the problem. Many problems can be solved remotely without any on-site intervention. In that case you wouldn't want your staff to respond, but would want to right source that function to a partner. If you have some less experienced, lower-cost staff, or interns, you may want them to do the first level of support, and only call the partner when it is time to escalate. There are usually two or three escalation levels set up, with another, highest, level that requires someone be dispatched to the location of the failed equipment with a spare part, and the proper configuration either already on the spare or readily available via that location. I am not talking about a help desk function for end users. We will cover that in the next chapter. This refers just to the reactive support for a network failure. As you work with your trusted partner to define how reactive support is handled, make sure your place in the escalation process is clearly articulated. You need to be made aware of any serious outage that affects your business. The contracts for such support are as varied as the possible support scenarios. The important thing is that your partner be able and willing to tailor the support contract, hours, service level, and costs to meet your needs and your budget.

Document, Document, Document

Every aspect of your backbone network must be thoroughly and accurately documented, right down to every line of configuration as we stated above, and every IP address. There is an even deeper level below the IP addressing that allows multiple sessions on a single address that is much too technical to cover here. We will touch on it when we talk about firewalls in Chapter 9.

Keeping up-to-the-minute accurate documentation is something every business struggles with. Detailed network documentation will include but may not be limited to:

◆ A global network map
◆ A diagram of each location
◆ A diagram of each device showing all connections
◆ Passwords to all devices

- All device configurations
- A logical map including all domains and IP addresses

You likely already have a network in place. It's just a matter of time before it has to be replaced. Start planning now if you didn't use this approach in the first place. You'll be far better off when the time comes. In fact, if you get this right, and then align your business strategy with your network infrastructure and applications, according to a study conducted by Momentum Research Group, you can potentially reduce your annual operating costs by more than 20 percent – and experience a 20 to 25 percent increase in customer satisfaction. Get it wrong, and you'll just bleed money in lost productivity and customer dissatisfaction.

Don't simply delegate these decisions to your IT staff. Be involved in the decision making process or at least review and understand these critical decisions as they are being made. It is too important to your business for you to simply delegate and ignore. As they say in the military, this information is treated on a need-to-know basis, and you need to know.

There are some standard designs for networks that are widely accepted in the IT industry. We mentioned that no two networks are alike, but there are some similarities and guidelines for network designs that are referred to as best practices. There are many best practice frameworks and approaches. The Information Technology Infrastructure Library (ITIL®) is the most popular. ITIL® or IT Infrastructure Library®, was developed by the UK's Office of Government Commerce as a library of best practice processes for managing IT.

ITIL® focuses on the business perspective of using IT solutions as a service to achieve business goals. That is the key to its popularity. Real change comes when you are able to change your viewpoint. The viewpoint of ITIL® is that Information Technology is a set of services (much like any utility) that is supplied to both internal and external customers. Only a service-centric model, that holds IT responsible for the ultimate quality and availability of these services, will enable organizations to achieve success.

ITIL® has typically been considered the standard for large organizations, but has recently released best practices for smaller companies. At the time of this writing ITIL® had just released ITIL® version 3. A web search on ITIL® reveals an extraordinary list of informational websites, most of them for firms consulting in the implementation of ITIL® best practices or offering books and guides for implementing this set of best practices. One organization, called the IT business edge, offers an ITIL® Starter Kit for small businesses that simplifies the voluminous information in ITIL® version 3 to help guide smaller businesses in the adoption of best practices. Their website is found at www.itbusinessedge.com. In the UK an organization called IT Governance Ltd. provides all kinds of ITIL® resources via their website at http://www.itgovernance.co.uk/itil.aspx.

One of the attractive things about the ITIL® standards is that you don't need to adopt the whole set of best practices at once to get the benefits. If your organization has not been following a specific best practices approach, you should seriously consider implementing them in a phased and/or selective approach. This is an approach that will take years, and is not to be lightly considered. You'll need to first get your staff trained. That means finding a firm in your area that does ITIL® training and consulting. Every aspect of IT and the critical decisions regarding IT that we discussed above can benefit from an ITIL® guided approach. Many companies start with just one aspect of their IT service delivery, and when they see the results, continue on a path towards adopting ITIL® best practices in all critical areas of their network. It is certainly worth exploring with your IT staff and trusted partner.

Summary

UGN's backbone requires careful planning and attention in order to effectively support the higher layers where the work of conducting business actually gets done. This chapter is by no means an exhaustive look at all the devices, software, configuration, documentation, security, and support issues that your IT staff deal with each day. It is meant to offer you a glimpse into their world, and some suggestions based upon experience, of the areas you should focus on as you take a vested interest in the health of UGN, your Utility Grade Network. As you inject yourself into the decision process resist the temptation to go down the many available "rabbit trails" that will get you bogged down in technical details. Leave the details to the experts, but make wise, informed decisions based on the impact on your business and the need to not just stop the bleeding that you are experiencing now, but to prevent future bleeding as well.

We've summarized the critical strategies, written plans/documentation, and the key areas of investment below.

Critical Strategies

- ◆ Standardize on one vendor
- ◆ Control access to all systems physically and logically
- ◆ Build in as much redundancy as you can afford
- ◆ Carefully store and guard all configurations
- ◆ Manage change closely
- ◆ Monitor all systems proactively
- ◆ Have a solid reactive support plan

Written Plans/Documentation

◆ Detailed network documentation
◆ Configuration management policy
◆ Change management policy
◆ Proactive and reactive support plans
◆ Clear escalation and notification policies
◆ Clearly documented best practices

Key Investments

◆ Top vendor's products with advanced/secure features
◆ Redundant hardware
◆ Backup Internet/WAN links
◆ Configuration management database software
◆ Asset management software
◆ Proactive monitoring
◆ Reactive support
◆ ITIL® training/consulting

Chapter 8

Server/PC and Peripheral Infrastructure

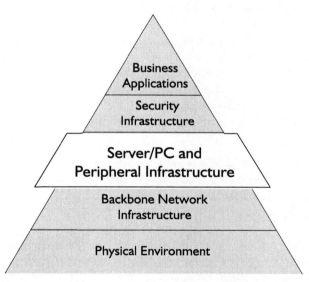

Now that we have covered what it takes to make sure that UGN's physical environment and backbone infrastructure are stable and secure, we can move up to the devices connecting to the backbone; the servers, PCs, laptops, and a host of other access devices and peripherals. If everything at this point functions at peak efficiency, these devices, that actually allow your workers to get things done, are much more apt to be the productive tools they are designed to be. Even still, there are a number of variables that can contribute to the performance of these devices, and the design, management and support of these variables can make all the difference, even on the most solid of backbone infrastructures in the most tightly monitored and controlled environments.

For the purpose of this discussion this layer consists of:

◆ Servers
◆ Storage
◆ Desktop/Laptop Computers
◆ Mobile Computing Devices
◆ Printers
◆ Other Peripherals (scanners, barcode readers, security cameras, etc.)

The objectives for keeping UGN healthy at this layer include:

◆ High Availability
◆ Data Protection
◆ Security
◆ Disaster Recovery

The last three objectives have often been lumped together under the objective of business continuity planning. An approach that incorporates high availability in daily operations is designed to take into account the major causes of unplanned downtime which are seemingly minimal human errors or minor disruptions that affect productivity. When viewed as a whole these are productivity killers that cost you dearly. Include them, and tightly weave all four of these objectives so that downtime is simply out of the question for your critical business resources. That is Utility Grade and makes for a very happy and healthy UGN.

You will attain these objectives using a strategy that includes:

◆ Written plans for High Availability, Data Protection, and Disaster Recovery (Chapter 9 will discuss a comprehensive security plan to include in this layer.)
◆ A solid design for each plan
◆ An effective help desk

It doesn't matter if you have ten employees, or 10,000 employees, you need to plan effectively for these systems to continuously operate at peak performance. Most companies do not, or they trust in one or two individuals to not only strategize, plan, and execute, but also to support their technology. We've made the case that this is extremely ineffective. As we discussed in Chapter 2, you need to form and engage a technology council. If your business is very small it just means you may need more people from outside the company to be on that council. The plan will be different for every company, but you need to have a plan. If you've had success with IT so far without a plan, beware. Someone is shooting arrows and then painting the bull's-eyes.

High Availability

Servers

The most critical part of your high availability plan is your servers. I am assuming that you have a LAN and that your LAN includes at least one server. It is possible to just connect a bunch of PCs to a switch and create a network without a server, which is really what my Rotary friend was referring to when he said he has a peer-to-peer network. If that's what you have, the way you work is a bit different from networks that have a server. You simply log onto your own computer, do your work, and if you need something that is on someone else's computer you can only get to it over the network if they have agreed to share it with other users on the network and have specifically given you permission to access it. This is pretty rare these days, but it is out there in some small businesses. In most environments you need a number of servers. Here are just a few of the many uses of servers:

Application Servers

These run the multitude of applications that run your business such as e-mail, accounting software, various business specific software like estimating software, proposal writing software, customer contact, sales forecasting, etc. Included are servers that run the programs required to run your network. We'll talk a little bit later about all that is going on behind the scenes just to make the various devices communicate with your servers and with servers out on the Internet. If you have an IP-based phone system, the software that runs your phones likely runs on servers as well.

File and Print Servers

To avoid all the sharing and permissions work on individual users' computers, these functions are centralized on dedicated file and print servers. If you print to a printer in your office that is not directly attached to your computer, chances are it is network attached and a server controls it.

Web Servers

Your website may be on your own web server inside of your network or it may be hosted on someone else's server. Either way there is a server running an application that displays your website and performs whatever level of functionality is designed into the site. In the latter case you are at the mercy of the host provider, and should assure the safety, security, and reliability of the environment and the provider company itself.

Security Servers

We've talked about Identity and Access Management (IAM). Your complete IAM solution is likely to include a number of servers that run the software that controls access to your network. You may also employ stand-alone "appliances" that are basically fixed function servers in a unique chassis, which are optimized for the particular function(s) they perform.

As you can see from the functions they perform, if your servers are not working your people are not working, it's that simple. Given how critical they are, it makes sense to assure that your servers are always available. This is not an area to scrimp on. You may be wondering, especially if you not at all technically inclined, just what the difference is between a regular desktop computer and a server. It is in the design of the components that are used in a server. A computer is a computer and they essentially have the same basic parts. Servers have a number of features built in to the hardware and software that make them more robust and more reliable. These are beyond the scope of this book. If you look at pricing models you'll see that a server is more expensive than a desktop PC with the same specifications in terms of processor, memory, storage, etc. You're paying for a higher level of reliability and it is well worth it.

As we discussed in Chapter 6 on the physical environment, your servers should be mounted in racks – preferably racks that are secured. As with your switches and routers, you face some important decisions with regard to your servers. We'll list a few here:

Equipment Vendor

Pick a single vendor and standardize. This cannot be overemphasized. It simplifies everything and proves more cost effective in the long term for all the same reasons that it does for all the areas of your network that we have already discussed.

Form Factor

We've already said that your servers need to be rack mounted. There are a number of designs. The most basic is a server like any other, except that its components are laid out is a very narrow horizontal chassis designed to slide into a rack on rails. These have actually come a long way. They are designed so that your technicians don't even need tools to snap on the sliding rails, or to open up the chassis in order to get to the various components for maintenance or upgrade purposes. A step up from that are blade servers. These offer a very compact design and the servers, as the name implies, are vertical blades that easily slide in and out of a chassis with power and cooling built into the backplane. The big four vendors, Dell, HP, IBM and Sun, constantly square off in tests for the best blade servers, and each seems to win their fair share of competitions. Compare features and prices then pick one of these and you won't go wrong.

Level of Redundancy

As with your physical infrastructure and backbone infrastructure, you need to decide what will happen when there is a failure in a server on your network. Fully redundant (mirrored) file servers each have the exact same information so that if one goes down the other can immediately assume its role. This type of 1:1 redundancy is expensive. Server clustering allows a number of servers to work together as nodes within the cluster so that if a single server goes down, any one of the others can assume its role. I'm not talking about a huge enterprise data center. Microsoft's Windows Server 2003 for example can work in clusters of up to eight servers. If complete server redundancy is not feasible due to cost considerations, it is important to at least design redundant power supplies and mirrored disk arrays, where any data can be stored on a number of disks in at least two locations for easy retrieval even if a single disk should fail. This is an intensely complex area and only those with experience designing and implementing redundant and/or clustered servers should be trusted to do so.

Storage

We talked a bit about storage above. Knowledge is power. Data provides knowledge. The problem today is often too much data. The amount of data being created and coming into your business is increasing at an alarming rate. The issue is not only how to store and access all of that data, but also how to protect it, from loss, theft, and corruption. Handling your data begins with how it is stored. There are a number of storage strategies, each with their own distinct advantages, limitations and corresponding costs. We aren't going to get into technical detail. Entire books are available on effective storage strategies and techniques. Basically though, there are three types of storage: *direct attached storage*: as in the hard drive in any computer; *network attached (NAS) storage*: stand-alone dedicated file servers or disk arrays; and the *storage area network (SAN)*: a pool of storage using interconnected storage devices and a common communication and control channel. How well any of these three perform is determined by the storage devices and the method of access to them. As we mentioned in the server section, you can design redundancy into whatever storage strategy is used. This is not a strong area of expertise for me. As I mentioned earlier, when our storage expert discussed our migration from a network attached storage model to a storage area network, he lost me in about ten minutes. This really is that technical. So I simple asked that he boil it down to just a few key questions. That is how you need to approach all of your technology decisions.

The first question was what was wrong with our existing strategy. The answer was that it couldn't easily grow with our expanding needs, and it was difficult to manage. The second question was what the benefits to the company would be if we invested in a SAN. The ability to rapidly and easily expand as our needs grew was just one advantage. There were many others. Improved speed when accessing data – always an issue in our high performance environment – was another advantage. That would improve productivity. The final question, and the one you most often ask, was how much it was going to cost. There was a significant up-front cost, but we would save money in the long run compared to continuing to add to our NAS. This made the decision very straightforward.

Stored data needs to be easily recovered or replicated in the case of a failure. As you store the incredible amounts of data that your business produces, the data needs to be backed up, either for your own needs in the event of a failure, or for compliance reasons. Data backup strategies vary depending upon how critical the data is, how much storage space you have available, and what, if any, regulations apply to your business. Backup and recovery programs allow for partial backups on a daily basis and full backups on a weekly basis, for example. If you backup periodically of course, you risk the loss of some data between backups. For more up-to-the-minute protection some solutions provide for continuous backup, usually establishing a base and backing up any changes in data immediately as they occur. Some solutions even allow end users to recover their own data via a web interface. This brings up a really difficult aspect of backup, the mobile user's laptop or hand-held device. In most cases, IT folks simply tell end users to save or upload any critical information to a file server so that it can be included in the automatic server backup.

The problem is that end users often do not know how or where to back up their data – a common result of insufficient communication and training. You need to either hold end user training that clearly identifies where and when to back up remote user data or invest in a solution that will automatically identify or point to the appropriate place or server on which desktop and laptop data should be backed up. Backup solutions exist that will automatically back up the data on the hard drive of a remote laptop if it is connected to the corporate network. This can be done by connecting to a high speed Internet connection, establishing a secure, encrypted tunnel (which we will discuss in more detail in the next chapter, Chapter 9, on security) and logging in to the corporate network. As long as the remote machine is adequately protected with personal firewall software, and the users are educated on the need and how to use the solution, they welcome the opportunity, much as they appreciate the automatic updates to anti-virus software that you should have in place, whenever they connect to the corporate network.

Speaking of data backup, e-mail is one particular area where you may be required to keep a complete history. Even if it is not required by regulation, it is a good practice to back up all of your e-mail and store it, in case you face litigation that requires an e-mail trail. With 80 percent of users saying e-mail is a more effective form of communication than the telephone and an estimated 90 percent of business communications occurring via e-mail, this can quickly become a storage nightmare. Nevertheless you need to include it in your data protection plan. There are some great solutions on the market that are specifically tailored for e-mail backup and archiving. Many of these solutions have built in compliance templates that will automatically enforce a variety of compliance adherence policies as the e-mail is stored for retrieval and is archived. In some instances individual user settings and mailboxes are regularly backed up and are quickly and easily restored in minutes – rather than the hours it might take manually.

On another note, you may want to control the use and content and security of instant messaging (IM). IM is gaining widespread use everywhere. Younger employees often use IM as their primary method of communication. You should establish policies for IM use during work hours, and may want to invest in a software solution to ensure compliance with those policies, should it become a problem.

As we mentioned in the last chapter, your servers/storage equipment connects to your core network infrastructure. Since these are the resources everyone is accessing, these need to be the most robust, reliable, and redundant connections in your network. By the way, not every server is connected on the same switch. Your web server(s) needs to be on an isolated section of the network for security reasons. Stealing from an old war term, we call that section of the network the DeMilitarized Zone (DMZ). Your DMZ sits outside of your corporate network and your firewall usually separates the DMZ and the corporate network. A possible exception is when you have web-based applications that your users access regularly. In that case you may have web servers on your corporate network, inside your firewall. There are about as many different configurations as you can imagine but those are the most basic. Protecting servers in the DMZ is particularly challenging, since those are the ones the public has access to. You may have heard about things like denial of service attacks, which flood web servers with so much bogus traffic that the server is rendered unavailable to legitimate users. Your backbone network strategy, discussed in the last chapter, must include protection from such attacks at the perimeter. Fortunately most vendors now build that type of protection into their equipment's operating system, either as a basic feature or as an add-on.

I hope you can see that laying this entire strategy out and making it work effectively is no small task. It takes a team approach of very bright people and not only technical people, but also those who will use the applications on your servers and the data being stored. As we mentioned in Chapter 2 your trusted partner should be able to bring in their own experts in this particular part of your network. One of your own IT people may be a master of this one thing. He still can't work in a vacuum and come up with a strategy that works for everyone.

Desktop/laptop PCs

As with your servers I strongly suggest that you standardize on a single manufacturer. You could use separate manufacturers for your laptop and your desktop PCs since these are very different form factors and there is no particular advantage or disadvantage either way. Standardized hardware and software configurations are a major plus from a support perspective. This is typically not an issue with desktop PCs. (This name has stuck from the days when the PC laid horizontally on the desk even though today most are towers that sit on the floor.) Since these are in the office, users tend to view them as company property and are less apt to mess with the configurations. Laptops are an entirely different story.

Laptops account for 82 percent of all new computer purchases, and these will often be used outside protected company firewalls. About 30 percent of users do not have personal firewalls on their laptops, and nearly 20 percent are not using antispyware. End users tend to treat these mobile systems as their own personal devices, often using them for extracurricular activities. The problem is that 35 percent of malicious software (malware) infections result from end-point intrusions while the system is off the corporate network. That's why you need to set, enforce, and measure compliance to your security plan, and deploy centrally managed anti-virus, anti-spam, client firewalls and intrusion detection. A known issue with anti-virus solutions is that the development of new malware precedes the development of the reactive code to detect and remove it. Anti-virus vendors have incredible networks of security experts around the world who are constantly on the look-out for new malicious code, so that they can distribute new updates to their customers as soon as possible. Still we read all the time of attacks that spread like wildfire and cause a lot of harm before they can be quarantined and removed. Client software is available that can detect any process that is running on a computer that has even a hint of the typical characteristics of malicious code. The software stops the execution of any code that seems suspicious. It doesn't need to know the exact nature of the code, or need to wait for an update that specifically recognizes the new threat. This software is more expensive than traditional anti-virus software, and while it prevents the code from executing and doing damage it doesn't remove it, which means it doesn't negate the need for anti-virus software to remove the code from the machine, or to block other, known viruses in the first place.

To manage the lifecycle of all of your PCs you should invest in an imaging and deployment solution. Operating system deployment, software distribution, and PC migration are just a few of the mundane tasks that your IT staff are required to perform on a daily basis. A variety of automated software packages are available that include features that efficiently streamline the work of your IT staff in managing the PC lifecycle while reducing support costs.

These systems pay for themselves in no time. Your IT staff is happier and more productive when you reduce their mundane tasks by allowing them to invest in automated tools. These tools also dramatically reduce human error - the number one cause of unplanned downtime. Have we said that enough times and in enough ways for it to sink in?

For those users who have laptops or who work from home an effective remote access strategy is essential. Most people have some form of high speed Internet access at home. In many cases this includes a wireless router. A little further on we'll talk about how to secure their connection into the corporate network. An effective remote access solution is one that allows them to do anything from home that they could do from a desk in the office. If you have an IP phone system they may be able to get voice mail messages in their e-mail. If they work extensively on the road like sales people and technicians tend to do, you may want to equip their laptops with a soft phone (software and a headset that plugs into their laptop so it essentially becomes their phone).

A major part of your high availability plan must include helping the end users who are typically not highly technical, and just want the tools they need to work all the time. That is the help desk's job. If your current help desk strategy is that a user calls or pages someone in IT and interrupts whatever he/she is doing at the time in order to get help, you are hurting your organization. 70 percent of the cost of end user computers is in the on-going support. It stands to reason that highly trained and competent technicians who are interrupted from very complex and intricate work on on-going projects to help a user whose child downloaded a new game onto her laptop which now somehow is making the laptop do "funny things", is going to be frustrated. That frustration comes right through the phone as the litany of basic questions begins. Add to it that the technician speak tech-ese while the extent of the end users technical vocabulary ends at "thumb-drive" and you can see why most end users give IT low grades for support.

If this even remotely describes your company's approach, you need to do one of two things to fix this: either engage your trusted partner to provide a basic help desk element, or bring in some top notch interns dedicated to your new help desk. The right interns are great. They work for next to nothing or even just for college credits. They are young, energetic, and looking to make their mark. These days they grew up with technology and probably know more about how to use it than most of your existing staff. They require a few key things: a very structured environment, a strong orientation program, inspirational leadership, and the right systems to do the job. If your IT staff is able to make the time investment in a strong intern program, with the right tools, it will pay huge dividends over time. You'll have a chance to cherry pick the cream of the crop as your organization grows. If they are hand-picked and trained to be polite and enthusiastic, and are given an escalation path for problems that go beyond their abilities, your end users will be delighted with the support.

The right tools include an electronic trouble ticket system that includes a solid knowledgebase that will grow to be an invaluable tool for solving most repetitive problems. A remote control strategy that allows a help desk technician to take over the remote PC is a must, along with the tools we mentioned above for distributing software updates, restoring applications and services remotely, and for assuring your protection mechanisms are installed, updated and running properly. Intel is now shipping PCs with these abilities built in to the computers processor chip. This technology even allows diagnostics on computers whose operating system is no longer functioning. I would strongly recommend that you never purchase another

PC of any kind for your company without this feature, keeping in mind the 70 percent figure above.

Getting back to the trouble ticket system – as soon as the call comes in a ticket is generated, the end user is given a ticket number, and then asked to describe the problem. The intern solves the problem quickly if possible, or gives an estimated call-back time. He/she researches the problem if it cannot be solved right away. If the intern finds a solution he/she quickly delivers it to the end user and if it works, the ticket is closed. If the intern cannot come up with a solid potential solution before the estimated call back time, the problem is escalated to a regular staff member. By this time, all the basic questions have been asked of the end user in a patient and polite way and the answers have been recorded in the ticket. Your staff technician is far more likely to be understanding, and if he/she fits the description of the right staff member for your IT organization described in Chapter 4, is likely to not only come up with a solution, but to also coach the intern in the process. This is great on the job training for your potential future full time staff member. Your staff will quickly recognize interns they would like to keep. As your organization grows and you need new staff members or someone to take the help desk leadership, you'll have some very solid candidates.

How do I know this works? We've been doing it for years. Many of our top engineers started as help desk interns. Over the years we've tweaked our help desk program to run like a well oiled machine, been hired to write an intern program for a local state college, and have established and taught a help desk curriculum at a local private college. This is all tremendously good for the local IT community, since highly trained interns make great employees at lots of other businesses. Being a stepping stone for interns is also a whole lot better than being a stepping stone for full time employees. If setting up an internal intern program is not feasible for your business, or just seems like too much work, then engage your trusted partner for help desk support. You will probably be helping them to groom some new interns. Be sure to check out their program, tools, and especially their escalation procedures to assure that they meet your standards for response to your end users. They will likely tailor the program to your specific needs.

Getting back to the user whose daughter loaded an infected game, this can be prevented at the outset. There are ways to lock-down end-user PCs so that new applications cannot be loaded by anyone other than an administrator. Most of these are manual procedures that are either inflexible, difficult to manage, or can be easily over-ridden. There are automated products that make desktop lockdown easy. One such product is made by a company called Bit9. It provides for centrally managed enforcement of rules for all types of applications running on PCs and laptops. It essentially allows you to establish a list of applications you will allow, and blocks all others from running – including all potentially malicious code. It is a whole lot easier and more effective than doing so manually.

Regardless of how you accomplish the help desk function, and what combination of manual and/or automated processes you use, measure the results. What gets measured gets attention. You should focus on the end user experience. Try to assess where you are in terms of availability of your critical resources. Keep track of every outage, every call ticket, and every escalation and get reports on them. Record the duration of outages and the number of users affected. Measure the average resolution time for call tickets. Measure end-user satisfaction levels on a regular basis. With the right strategy, procedures, tools, and equipment you will see dramatic improvements over time. You will slow or even stop the bleeding from lost productivity. Your IT staff and your end users will be much happier. Life really will be good.

Data Protection

A lot of what we have already said above includes various aspects of data protection. For the purpose of this section we will focus on controlling access to your data and assuring that the data does not get into the wrong hands. I mentioned the idea of locking down a PC to assure that only certain approved programs are allowed to be installed or to run on it. It is also possible to prevent the copying of data files that are marked as protected, onto any type of portable storage device. That is one way to control data leakage at the PC level.

The most fundamental way of protecting data on your network is by setting up access rights for each user as the user's credentials are established. If you have a LAN with a server, the server exists on what is referred to as a domain. Each domain is a collective set of resources, and anyone who is given credentials with which to enter that domain can utilize those resources. There is a practical limit to the size of a domain and you may also want to limit the particular domain to only a few specific users in order to isolate access to certain resources to just those users. For those reasons many businesses have several domains. If you are using Microsoft Windows and are logging in to a domain, the name of the domain will show up on your log in screen. If you are not attached to a domain, you can still sign on to your local PC. That is as technical as we're going to get here, and I said all of that just to point out that there is some basic protection of data inherent in any network that requires a user to log in. We discussed that some servers are used simply to store data files. To break it down a little further, the storage locations are uniquely identified, and in your user credentials you need permission to access those specific locations. So if you were to attempt to access data in a location that you did not have permission to access, you would get an error message basically telling you that you don't have access rights to that location. Since you're the boss you may not have seen such a message.

This all seems very good and very secure. Setting it all up and keeping track of it though, is extremely complicated and time consuming – like a lot of what we have discussed. And, as sharp as the people who write the software and implement it are, there is an ever present hacker community looking to get into those protected places to either destroy, corrupt, or steal that data just for kicks. In addition, there are often some equally bright people inside of businesses who simply want to get to information not intended for them, such as salary information. The first and simplest data protection is to require that passwords be changed on a regular basis. Password cracking software is readily available on hacker sites on the Internet, so without strong protection it is easy to crack a password and get into a system. Once inside a domain the potential thief has access to any locations the actual owner of the login credentials has. And of course, those with administrative rights, who set all this up, can go anywhere. Individual files can be password protected; like a spreadsheet in Excel can be by using the permissions capability inherent in MS Office. This will slow a hacker down but can also be cracked. An even greater level of protection would be to encrypt the file and lock it down with password credentials or even two factor authentication. Two factor authentication means that the user has a token which generates a random number sequence that is time sensitive, and has a memorized pin number. Only by entering both numbers as the password, is access granted. This is extremely secure, but is not only an expensive solution, it is extremely cumbersome to the end user if every important file is encrypted and requires this type of authentication.

For that reason I suggest that you use two-factor authentication any time you are going to allow a user to access your network from outside the company. Securing a virtual private connection into your network (VPN) is critical. To establish a VPN connection there is software installed on the user's machine that attempts to launch a connection into your network. Since the established connection is allowed to go through your firewall, and directly into your network, where the user will be allowed to enter a domain, it is referred to as a tunnel. The process of establishing one of these tunnels obviously has to be extremely well protected. It starts by prompting the user to log in to the tunnel, a separate process from actually logging onto the network. This log in process should be set up to require two factor authentication. After the tunnel is established the user is logged into the network as they would be from inside the network. If a laptop is stolen that is equipped for VPN access, and the process is only secured by a password, a tech-savvy individual can get in. Even with two-factor, though, if your user keeps the token in their laptop bag with the pin number written on the back they defeat the purpose. Don't laugh, I've seen it.

The greatest degree of data vulnerability for many companies is e-mail on laptops. A laptop with a password as its only defense is pretty vulnerable. As simple password cracking routine will likely get in. Once an unauthorized user is inside, even if there are no sensitive files stored there, and you have some solid protections, like two-factor authentication to prevent access to the corporate network, e-mail is usually wide open. Any messages that have already been downloaded can be readily viewed. A lot of very sensitive data is communicated via e-mail. Unless you prohibit the use of e-mail for sensitive communications – which is generally impractical, you should insist that sensitive e-mail be encrypted. This is not an easy pill to swallow, and the large majority of companies will simply ignore the issue and hope for the best. E-mail encryption is expensive, and is only effective if it includes strong authentication.

Strong authentication in this case means a digital certificate stored on a portable device like a thumb drive, or the previously mentioned token authentication. This is a good lead in to the ongoing topic of security.

Security

Security must be tightly woven into every part of UGN's hierarchy at every level, as you can tell from the discussions above. That is why the next chapter is entirely dedicated to security. We don't suffer from paranoia, although it might appear that way. There are very real threats. Unlike other utilities, your utility grade network is a constant target. Small- to medium-size businesses actually invest a larger percentage of their overall IT budget into security than larger companies. This is largely due to the fact that a larger portion of the cost of scalable security solutions is in the basic system itself. Per-user costs decline with the higher numbers of users. As we will see in the next chapter, you need an overall security plan that encompasses all areas of your network. For your server, PC, and peripheral layer specifically, if you control access to the network using two-factor authentication, and then use strong passwords for any data you want to protect on the inside (along with a well designed and enforced resource access strategy) you should be in good shape. Encrypting individual files is necessary only for extremely sensitive data. Remember the data on laptops in particular in that case – a lot of laptops are stolen each year especially during travel. I've been there – fortunately I do use two factor authentication, store no highly sensitive company information locally, and protect mildly sensitive data with strong passwords. You would be wise to do the same.

Disaster Recovery

There are a number of reasons for the statistics presented in Chapter 6 regarding the reasons so many companies who experience a disastrous fire never re-open. You do need to be prepared for a disaster of any kind. I personally believe it is your civic duty to be prepared in the case of a terrorist attack affecting your business. It is critical for whatever reasons. If access to your critical applications is interrupted for a prolonged period your business may actually bleed to death.

You can see from the complexity of the information we have discussed at this layer, that it would be nearly impossible to rebuild your server infrastructure from scratch in a reasonable period of time. Instead you have to have a well thought out plan that is in force at all times should the unspeakable ever occur. At this layer the plan must include details of how you are going to recreate your server infrastructure, restore all of your critical applications on that infrastructure, restore your critical data associated with each of these applications, and restore your users' access to those systems.

Much of what we've discussed with regard to redundancy and the like, applies inside your data center. If that data center is destroyed, most of those systems will go with it. It is not often practical for small to medium businesses to engage with large firms that provide off-site disaster recovery services. I think it helps to keep in mind that every piece of information in IT systems is stored as a series of ones and zeroes. Each is referred to as a bit of information. If you can store every bit of information somewhere off site, then you just need another physical location to put that information, that closely resembles the location all those bits came from, and you will be able to restart business quickly. At its lowest level it is not all that complex.

We have already establishes that you can store a copy of all your applications, and all of your application related data. You can also store a copy of all of your configuration data. This configuration data should also include exactly how your LAN, your domain(s), your user profiles, your remote access, your firewall(s), etc. are set up. Armed with this information, given you have a potential site from which to operate, you have the ability to recover from a disaster. A multitude of companies emerged as a result of the bursting of the dot com bubble, which left a lot of unused capacity in some very large data centers. In many cases, the companies that originally owned these data centers went out of businesses because their investors stopped pouring money in to them when they realized this glut of capacity was not going to be utilized any time soon. The data centers were sold for pennies on the dollar. All that capacity was now in the hands of people who had bought it on the cheap. Thus emerged a number of companies who rent space on their servers, where you can store what amounts to a mirror image of your critical servers and applications. Many of them also allow you to store back-ups of critical data. Money was no object when many of these data centers were built, so the best state of the art products were used. The NCPI in these data centers is astounding. The security is also amazing, and the monitoring and management systems are often the best available in the IT industry.

A quick on-line search of disaster recovery services yields a litany of available solutions. We don't recommend any one in particular. They are a bargain, and your disaster recovery strategy should include such a vendor.

But what happens to your workers. That is a bit more difficult. There is some really good news though. The 82 percent figure regarding how you've been investing in end user PCs is really going to help you if your company has been equipping them with laptops. Granted laptops are more expensive than desktops, and we have already discussed that they are more difficult to secure, control, update, and maintain. This makes the total cost of ownership even higher. The silver lining is that your workers can not only extend the work day to increase productivity, they can work from anywhere if disaster strikes. You can have them work from home. You can fly them all to a hotel in Hawaii that has high speed Internet (just kidding). They can gather at Starbucks or the airport. Since they do 90 percent of their communication via e-mail, as long as your e-mail system is restored you are in pretty good shape from an IT perspective. If you use an IP-phone system, and their laptops are equipped with a soft phone you are ready to resume much of the other ten percent of communications.

If you are not quite that modern an operation, and you use a traditional phone system along with a lot of desktop machines, you should still engage a disaster recovery company for your servers, applications, and data. Your plan in that case has to include a physical location for your users to go to with phones and desktop PCs. If you have invested in automated software for imaging and software deployment the process of loading up these machines will take less time than it will take for you to get the necessary communication lines and Internet access into the temporary location. Some areas of the country offer physical disaster recovery sites that already have circuits, phone systems, and even PCs. Have your IT staff do some research on what is available for inclusion in your disaster recovery plan.

Your plan has got to be tested periodically. Having a written well thought out and researched plan does you little good if Murphy shows up – and you know he will – when disaster strikes. If you never actually test the plan there is a good chance that it won't work as planned. You have to iron the kinks out, and the only way to do that is with testing. You also have to update the plan after each test. How often you test the plan depends on factors such as the extent to which your company relies on IT, the regulations your company must comply with, the area of the country you live in, etc. I've even heard it said that investors valuating companies look at the disaster recovery capability as one factor in the valuation. This is just another way in which wise investment in IT might pay off.

Summary

Keeping UGN healthy at level 3 (servers, PCs, and peripherals) requires wise planning and investing. We'll summarize the critical strategies, written plans, and the key areas of investment below.

Critical Strategies:

- ◆ One vendor each for servers, PCs, laptops
- ◆ Standardize configurations
- ◆ Built-in redundancy for servers, storage
- ◆ Regular backup of all critical data
- ◆ Regular full restoral testing
- ◆ Automation of routine tasks
- ◆ Help desk right-sourcing or interns

Written Plans:
- High Availability
- Data Protection
- Disaster Recovery
- Security (see next chapter)

Key Investments:
- Rack-mount servers with some level of redundancy
- Automated life-cycle management tools
- Solid storage infrastructure
- Automated backup/restoral tools
- Effective remote access with two-factor authentication
- Help desk tools
- Disaster recovery solution

Chapter 9
Security Infrastructure

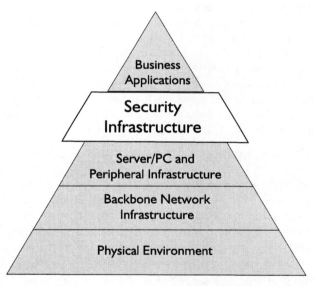

Up to this point, the layers we have discussed in UGN's hierarchy of needs formed the building blocks of your hardware network. Integral to each of these layers is the protection of each system. Security considerations are both physical and logical. We discussed some of the physical considerations in Chapter 4 when discussing the physical environment. We will also include physical security in parts of our discussions in this chapter. The logical considerations center around software itself, and the access to the various types of software on your network, be they device configurations or business applications. All of these physical and logical security systems are collectively referred to as your security infrastructure.

I don't believe we can overstress the importance of security for your business. It is an area that is not getting the attention it requires. Look at these disturbing facts regarding security implementations in small to medium businesses according to AMI, an IT research firm in New York:

◆ About 82 percent of small business and 64 percent of medium sized businesses have no security management.

◆ 75 percent of small businesses and 50 percent of medium sized businesses don't have identity and access management either.

◆ Roughly 60 percent of small and 45 percent of medium businesses have no patch management or encryption.

◆ 64 percent of small and 45 percent of medium sized businesses have experienced a malicious electronic attack in the past year.

It's no wonder that 73 percent of IT managers fear that they may lose their job due to a severe security breach, and 62 percent say these worries affect their personal lives. Technology market research company Vanson Bourne polled almost one thousand UK and US IT decisions makers, and found that the worst culprits of security breaches are junior sales people. These men and women, between the ages of 26 to 35, are multi-taskers and tech savvy, using applications such as e-mail, instant messaging, VoIP, and the web, in any combination, without considering the potential dangers. The report shows that the best behaved regarding security matters are also the most knowledgeable: the techies. These were middle-management males, between the ages of 26 to 35, who work within the technology function. Their research revealed the internal weaknesses small businesses are facing in trying to manage external threats.

The news is full of constant reports of new and creative threats to any company's network. In an April 2007 editorial feature, *Messagewire*, an on-line e-mail security magazine details some new and old information. They reported that hackers are increasingly creating fake browsers to deceive users and direct Internet traffic. With fake browsers and other malicious code, they can gain control of computers by tricking the user. Users can also fall victim to data and identity theft or violations of privacy when using rogue browsers. *Messagewire* indicated that FaceTime, another e-mail security reporting service issued a warning to the IT community after discovering that NetBrowserPro, a web browser promising secure porn browsing, instead installs a rootkit – a set of tools intended to conceal running processes, files or system data from the operating system, often giving hackers administrative or super-user access to the underlying operating system. Two big problems here: first; users should not be trying to load anything to do with pornography on a company-owned computer, and second; the rootkit allows third party applications to interact with the browser. Many of the photo galleries linked from the browser will redirect the end-user to an unintended location, which is potentially a security threat.

That same article referred to a report issued by Commtouch Software indicating that an old e-mail-borne worm, known as Bagle or Beagle had celebrated its third birthday by continuing to defeat most anti-virus solutions with its cleverly-devised distribution method. At the time the worm used key offensive strategies to maximize propagation and slip under the radar of traditional anti-virus defenses.

An attack on Linux web servers in January 2008 placed malicious code on over 10,000 servers that attacked the PC of users accessing the sites, and exploited known vulnerabilities in programs like Quickbooks, and even Yahoo Messenger. There is no telling how many millions of machines were attacked by the time this book hits print.

The federal government has not been immune to brandjacking, the hijacking of an organization's brand. Online fraud scams have spoofed federal organizations such as the Better Business Bureau and the IRS, as well as government agencies on every level – federal, state and local.

Even IT vendors are struggling with security issues according to a survey by consulting giant Deloitte. Almost half – 49 percent – of the over 100 companies surveyed in their 2007 Technology, Media & Telecommunications Security Survey say they are "falling behind or catching up to security threats." Just seven percent believe they are ahead of them.

The report also found that only 54 percent have a formal information security strategy while 17 percent of the surveyed companies see the lack of such a strategy as one of their biggest barriers to achieving information security. 45 percent say top management is "informed about security issues only on an ad hoc basis or not at all." Obviously they need to do better, and so do you.

I did say in the Introduction that fear is not a compelling motivator. Allow me to suggest that in this case you should be fearful, and that fear must motivate you to action. The question is what to do about all this.

Security Strategy

First and foremost your company needs a comprehensive written security strategy. If you do not have one, that is the place to start. Cisco Systems offers an automated tool on their website called the security policy builder that actually creates a security policy template for your company after asking just a few specific questions. The tool automatically e-mails the template to you after you complete the short questionnaire on line. I tried it and it provides a solid foundation to start from if you have never done a written security plan. To use the tool visit: www.ciscowebtools.com/spb/

If you do have one, you need to examine its effectiveness. Is it up to date with current security risks? Can it scale with your organization? Are there more effective/cost-effective strategies that have emerged since it was written? Have you already outgrown it? And the big question: Is it effectively enforced? Your first step in formulating an effective company wide security strategy is to assess what you have.

You already have some security in place even if you don't have a written plan. Take stock of what you have, what it is intended to protect, and how well protected you feel that you are in that area.

Do you have:

- ◆ A firewall either stand-alone or embedded in each router.
- ◆ VPN security on all internal data going across the public network.
- ◆ An intrusion detection and prevention system.
- ◆ Anti-X (virus, spam, spyware, phishing, etc.).
- ◆ Wireless security for any wireless connectivity.
- ◆ Desktop and/or e-mail encryption.
- ◆ Strong identity management/two factor authentication.
- ◆ Compliance assurance and validation where applicable.

It is clear that you understand the risks associated with e-mail. Almost every company surveyed employs anti-virus, spam filtering, and spyware protection. Since much, if not most, of your company's communication is via e-mail, it makes good sense that you would protect that first. Nice job. If you can do as well with the rest of your security infrastructure your IT manager will be more apt to sleep at night.

Again the question is not just whether you have these systems in place, but also how well are they protecting you? To determine how well protected you are, you may need an outside company to actually test your security. Just because you haven't been attacked or infected doesn't guarantee that you are not vulnerable. You may have just been lucky so far. Your trusted partner should be well versed in security, and must either be able to assess and test these systems for you or be associated with additional outside resources whom they trust to do the assessment and report the result. Armed with your assessment information you can effectively start on your written plan.

Security is entirely about mitigating risks to your business. You need to understand and evaluate the risks associated with your particular business. It is an arduous task, but it is worth the effort to try to understand the financial impact of the various risks in order to map out your security plan, and to invest wisely in your security infrastructure. The list of questions you need to ask can be extensive, depending on the business you are in, the sensitivity and/or value of the information you store, the compliance issues you face and possible impact of non-compliance, and the potential impact of any type of breach to your customers and to your reputation.

A few things you should consider include:

- ◆ The potential financial impact of a network outage due to a security breach.
- ◆ The potential disruption of your supply chain.
- ◆ How long your website could be down before you suffered significant financial impact.

◆ If you are engaged in e-commerce, how long your storefront could be down before you suffered a significant financial impact.

◆ The impact of failing to comply with regulations that pertain to your business, not just in potential fines but in the man-hours it will take to resolve any deficiencies.

I'm sure your team will come up with other issues to consider. The point is you have to understand the risk you face, and invest accordingly to mitigate it. Now that you have assessed where you are, and the risks your company faces, you need to develop a protection strategy in the form of a written network security plan.

It is important to take an outside-in layered approach to network security. As we go through some of the key areas of your network security plan you should be looking at the big picture from the perspective of who or what can potentially harm you. This should start with those outside of your network. How might someone from the outside get in or do damage? They could attack a web server by flooding it with so many bogus sessions that no legitimate sessions can be established. As the results imply, this is referred to as a denial of service attack. They could hijack a connection into your network that one of your remote users has established over an unsecured wireless link. Once on that connection they have as much access inside your systems as the authorized user. This is the first layer you must protect – the outside layer also referred to as the perimeter. Protecting the perimeter is sometimes referred to as network access control (NAC) which simply means controlling who can gain access into your network.

A second layer would be the systems inside your network. If someone does penetrate whatever defenses you've established outside your network, or is a guest on your inside network, you have to control where they can go. In addition your employees, customers, consultants, and others may be granted access inside your perimeter. What is their job function or their purpose in gaining access? How are you going to control where they go and what resources they use? This can be done in a lot of different ways. You can segment parts of your network physically, although this creates more challenges than it solves. You can segment your network logically, which requires that your backbone equipment support these features. We looked at one strategy in Chapter 7 when we discussed the concept of virtual LANs. Without getting too technical it involves the management of what resources a user attached to an interface on a device, or using a particular computer, can access. We looked at another strategy when we talked about domains in Chapter 8. A user assigned to a particular domain (set of resources) may or may not have access to another domain. Even then a user's profile may limit access to particular resources in the domain, like files stored on a particular storage device for example.

A third layer would be actual data. Even if a user can get to a storage device, data on that device could be password protected, like our spreadsheet example, or it could actually be encrypted. File encryption is gaining in popularity due to the sensitive nature of financial, health, and personal information and the growing regulations regarding the storage and handling of such information. Access to data should be on a need-to-know basis. Most people take an opposite view. Everyone gets to see everything unless there is a specific reason why they should not. The potential for exposure is far greater in that approach. View all of your data as precious company property and only allow access to those who have a specific reason for viewing that data. Besides your people, your data is likely your most valuable asset.

Whatever the layers, and how you protect them, the important thing is that you take a layered approach, and you secure each layer in the most appropriate and cost-effective way for your company. You will be most effective in doing so with a well thought out written plan.

Your network security plan should do the following.

Physically protect your IT assets

When we discussed the Physical Environment within your data center and at the intermediate distribution points in your network, we talked about the fact that you need to control access to these devices. This physical security strategy needs to be tightly integrated into your overall security plan. Your data center, regardless of where it is physically located or how it is configured, should be locked, and access to it restricted to those who are both authorized and qualified to work on it. In an optimal configuration, your core network equipment is stored in locked racks so that access is further limited to select people in your IT group – assuming you have a group of IT people. One of the worst threats to your network is actually a disgruntled employee or ex-employee. I remember being on-site for a large implementation at AT&T in Maitland, Florida when I was working for Motorola in the early 80s. They had a major layoff, and critical systems started to fail unexplainably. They had an immediate lock-down in their data center and I suddenly had to be escorted inside by one of two particular individuals. One of the unfortunate drawbacks to the fact that many IT folks don't really understand business, and what it really takes to attain and maintain profitability, is that this lack of understanding sometimes translates into a disdain for senior management. You have to protect your business from those who have access to critical systems who become disgruntled or leave your company for whatever reason. There must be a well defined procedure that is swiftly invoked and extremely thorough at revoking their physical and logic access rights.

Protect your network from internal and external attacks

This is not a simple matter at all. The types of attacks are varied and can target just about every device in your network. The ones mentioned at the beginning of this chapter are just a very few of all the potential threats. I've mentioned that even the operating code of your routers and switches has flaws that are uncovered and could be exploited on a regular basis. The same holds true for your servers and

PCs. In addition, laptops make up a large percentage of computers in today's highly mobile workforce. Your users tend to view their laptops as personal devices, often using them for non-business related purposes in the home. If steps are not taken to prevent it, they often load non-business related applications on laptops, sometimes directly from non-trusted Internet sources. If you allow guests on the network, you face similar issues from their machines. I mentioned in the last chapter that software is available to manage the configuration of, and to "scrub", every machine that connects to your network.

Malicious code is developing at the fastest pace in history. Even if you have an effective anti-virus strategy, new viruses come out before the fix for them does, and are proliferated around the world literally in seconds. Anti-virus strategies offer a great deal of protection, but are sometimes reactive solutions. Fortunately proactive technology exists to stop the execution of any software that looks like it is doing something suspicious on a computer. This software can quarantine the suspect code before it does any damage and hold it until it is determined to be safe or not. One such solution is offered by Cisco Systems and is called Secure Agent. It is not inexpensive, but it is further protection from malicious code and could easily pay for itself by protecting all of your computers from just one malicious incident. Get a clear understanding of what you have and how well it protects you, and then decide if you are willing to invest more heavily to get higher protection levels.

Intel is even putting code on their processors that allows secure remote management, updating, and troubleshooting of a PC, as was mentioned in the previous chapter. You don't necessarily need to buy the software either. We'll talk in the final chapter about such rapidly advancing software-as-a-service offerings as well as managed service offerings that you can subscribe to in order to mitigate risks without huge up-front investments.

Protect your network from intrusion

Network intrusions occur as a result of the exploitation of existing vulnerabilities in network devices and security systems. One of the favorite pastimes of the hacker community is to try to invade, or hack into, company networks. There are thousands of websites, blog sites, forums, etc. where information on vulnerabilities and how to exploit them are openly discussed and shared. Bragging rights belong to the one who is able to break into the largest network, the most secure network, the largest number of networks in a given time period, etc. Sometimes the objective is to steal information, more often though, it is simply to take down or alter a website.

We mentioned in the last chapter that your website, including e-commerce if applicable, will reside in a separate section on the network that is easily accessible to the public. That also makes it a sitting duck if you don't protect it. Fortunately most routers have features either built into the basic operating system or available as an add-on which protect from the myriad of intrusion techniques in use. There are always new innovations here as well, so periodic updates of the operating system need to be applied. Your trusted partner who provides this equipment should also alert you whenever an update is released, and advise you as to whether it applies to your particular implementation.

Everyone knows about the need for a firewall. An effective strategy should include a redundant firewall and may include a number of firewalls. Fortunately routers for branch offices and for small businesses include firewall capability. We discussed in some detail how the whole process of IP addressing works and the fact that there are public and private addresses. You may wonder how we can control where a user goes as they come through the firewall. There are many processes required to do even the simplest task that we take for granted. Networks use a layered approach so taht all of it works properly.

The physical connections are the lowest layer and it works up from there. The IP addressing that we talked about is also a low level process. On top of that process is a more complex protocol that controls how an application, like your browser for example, can actually request access to a web page. The web page is an application running on a server. At this next level up, referred to as the transport layer, and controlled by the transport control protocol (TCP) an actual session is requested by your browser, once it has established the IP address of the server (remember the DNS function?). TCP controls the process of delivering the request for opening a session with the website on the server, and the delivery of the acknowledgement of that request. TCP uses port numbers to identify common application on the network and to establish connections for the use of those applications. Web browsing is generally a very non-threatening function, with a standard port number. In order for a web browsing session to come into your network, your firewall needs to be set up to allow that type of session through. This is referred to as opening a port. There are some functions that only trusted employees can use because their improper use can be very dangerous.

The firewall must be configured to stop all types of sessions except for those that are non-threatening. This is referred to as locking down the network. If it were only that simple your IT staff would have little to worry about. The trouble is that hackers continuously invent new ways to fake out the firewall or the routers. One way is to disguise one type of potentially destructive session as if it were another, harmless session. This is called spoofing. Another way is to intercept, or hijack a session.

The possibilities are numerous. Fortunately the good guys keep coming up with ways to foil the villains. Operating systems are designed to look for common intrusion methods and stop them before they get in, and to alert you when this occurs. Intrusion detection and prevention systems have proven to be complex and hard to manage. They are constantly improving though, and are a very necessary part of your network security system.

If you want to maintain the security of your systems and better protect them from malicious attacks, then you should think about attacking your own network in order to do so, according to Ron Nguyen, a Director of Consulting for McAfee, a leading network security and management provider.

"If they don't hack their network, the attackers are going to hack first," said Nguyen, who teaches a class called "The Essentials of Hacking" for users to get a better perspective of what techniques, tools and methodologies attackers are using. He notes a lot of companies are implementing automated tools that assist in testing but also recommends that it be paired up with a professional third party that would also perform an assessment to ensure everything is all right. Your security plan should include regular assessment of the vulnerability of your network to malicious attacks. Vulnerability scanning is available in many network management systems and regular vulnerability scanning should be an integral part of your security plan.

Protect the privacy of your communications at all times across all links

Regardless of whether your users are in a remote office, at home, or sitting in Starbucks on a wi-fi connection, any information they are sending or receiving directly from your corporate network across the public network needs to be encrypted. If the user is in a remote office you may have a private connection, which does ensure privacy. If that office connects via the Internet, chances are you are using a virtual private network (VPN) secure tunnel. The VPN connection is typically handled by the routers on both ends of the link, and all user data between the routers is encrypted and encapsulated in secure data packets – thus forming what appears as an impenetrable tunnel. If the user is a single computer connected to the Internet, there needs to be software on that computer that performs a similar encryption and tunneling function. This is fairly standard practice today and was described in the last chapter's discussion on laptop PCs. It should be noted that a wireless router in the home is often left wide open. You should insist that if your users work from home on a wireless router, they protect wireless connections with a security code. You should have your IT staff train your users in how to do so. It isn't difficult, and many may have already done so, but for those who haven't the class will be informative, will help secure your network, and could build some good will between the end users and IT staff – if it is done in a friendly informative way.

Control access to information based on pre-determined rights

We can break down access control into four basic areas:

◆ **Authentication**: Is the user indeed who they claim to be? Where are they coming from?

◆ **Access**: What areas of the network is this user allowed to access?

◆ **Authorization**: What resources in these areas is the specific user authorized to use?

◆ **Accounting/Auditing/Monitoring**: It is important to know and to track user activity.

The most basic form of access control is, of course, user name and password. If this is the extent of your access security you need to at least make sure that you require regular changing of passwords, that the passwords include some number(s)/special character(s), and that your users are not allowed to have a sticky note attached to the computer with that information on it. There are people who do that in just about every company I've ever been to. This is a matter of training your employees, which we'll discuss further.

For higher security at the office and/or for remote users you can implement digital certificates – which are basically a set of credentials that are pre-issued to particular users and are stored either on their computer or on a thumb drive or similar device. The distribution of these certificates must be tightly controlled, and certificates of employees leaving the company must be immediately revoked. Again, the investment in the technology is relatively small, the on-going management, which must be spelled out in your security plan, is where most of the costs lie. There are services your company can subscribe to in order to issue and control the use of digital certificates. These often prove more cost effective than investing in your own in-house solution. Clearly define the intent of having the certificates, the controls associated with the issuance, the access rights of particular users or groups of users, the life-cycle and revocation of certificates, and management rights and responsibilities. Present them to potential outsource services to determine how well they meet your needs. You can then make an informed decision to outsource the service or do it in-house. Once again though, if your choice is to perform the service in house, you have to evaluate your staff's ability and experience, and engage your trusted partner as necessary.

You can provide even higher security with two factor authentication. In that case the user has a device known as a token, which generates a new password in the form of a numeric code – referred to as a pass-code, at regular intervals. The user is prompted to enter a memorized pin number, along with the pass-code, to form the full password that allows him into your system. The two factors are the PIN; what you know, and the token; what you have (as proven by your knowledge of the current pass-code). This is a very secure way to control access to critical systems. Let me emphatically state here, that these systems are only as good as the policies for use that are part of your security strategy, and how well you enforce them. The Business Performance Management (BPM) Forum conducted a survey in which almost 60 percent of respondents have said that they have shared their network password with a colleague and 17 percent had either given out or received someone else's token or smart card. That is the result of a lack of training and enforcement, and is management's responsibility to correct.

Of course all of this information is just to get a user signed on. Once signed on, the user should have access only to the information and applications necessary. That is controlled by the access rights associated with their login credentials, as we discussed in the last chapter regarding user domains. An important part of your security strategy has to be the clear definition of who gets access to what and when. Much of the application of compliance regulations as they relate to IT focus on this particular issue, and the tracking of daily usage. You can also set up a Virtual Local Area Network (VLAN) which ensures that a user, either by virtue of the machine he is using or of his login credentials, can only get access to particular servers. We used the case of your finance people in Chapter 6.

In large organizations with thousands or even tens or hundreds of thousands of employees, there are highly sophisticated systems referred to as Identity and Access Management (IAM) systems. These systems automate most of the processes we've just described. Think about your on-line banking or web purchasing experiences. If you have ever created your own sign-on credentials, and then forgotten either your user name or password, it is likely that in attempting to sign on with the wrong password, the system gave you an error message. Then the system gave you a way to solve the problem on your own, maybe by answering a few security questions, and then sending your password to your e-mail. This is not what happens to a user who forgets his password in a small company. That user has to talk to an administrator who either manually assists in the password recovery process, or resets the user's password to a default value, or even changes the user's password for them. Depending on the number of disparate systems that require log-on, and the number of users, a lot of skilled IT staff time is wasted on such mundane tasks. As you approach the issue of access control you want to use the same type of IAM mind-set in your security plan. Even if you cannot afford or don't need a sophisticated automated system, you need to look at it from a business operation standpoint that takes account of the productivity impact of completely manual, disparate systems. There are three broad functional areas to consider:

a. **Identity administration and provisioning**. How does/will your organization manage user identities, and the process associated with the creation, modification, suspension or deletion of user accounts and entitlements on all of your IT systems.

b. **Access Management**. How does/will your organization control access to all of your critical resources including systems, system files and databases, and various applications.

c. **Auditing and Monitoring**. How does/will your organization track and report identity and access, changes, and usage activity across the network.

You can take gradual steps that include a system that allows users to sign on once and gain access to many or all of the applications they need. Single sign-on solutions are available and are not prohibitive expensive, and may provide the auditing and monitoring capabilities you want, or that your company needs due to compliance regulation.

So far we have focused on access to systems. Depending upon how critical your information is, you may want or need to drill down to the data level, and protect individual data files using encryption. The most basic form is the password protection that is available with Microsoft Office. It is common, for example, for managers to password protect a financial spreadsheet that is sent to a colleague via e-mail. A subsequent e-mail is sent with the password to unlock the spreadsheet. A comprehensive system for completely locking down access to your data at every point in your network, and controlling every piece of information in and out of your servers is possible using powerful – and expensive – data governance products. If you have extremely sensitive client data, or research data, or if you have extremely tight compliance issues, stringent data governance must be a part of your security strategy. One such product is offered by a company called Veronis. They offer a great white paper entitled "10 steps to preventing data loss" on their website at www.veronis.com. I am not necessarily endorsing their product or suggesting its applicability to yours or anyone else's business. I just like the way they present the information in that particular white paper and think it is worth a read. I should note that security studies reveal that very few small to medium sized companies protect data on laptops with anything but a simple Windows sign on, even when their sales people and executives travel regularly. The number of laptops stolen at airports is significant to be sure, but even more alarming is the fact that the data on those laptops is not protected. Your security plan should not only identify what information may be stored on laptops, but must also identify and set standards for enforcing data protection on any sensitive company data that you allow on laptops. You should start with your own laptop.

Assure adherence to any compliance requirements associated with your business

Compliance is a major issue in an increasing number of industries today. Financial and healthcare companies in particular have stringent compliance standards for which they are regularly audited. It is beyond the scope of this book to get into the details of the various regulations and standards. We will take a very cursory view of just a few of the current standards that have had a tremendous impact on the IT industry in recent years.

The Payment Card Industry Data Security Standard (PCI DSS)

PCI DSS began with each credit card issuer establishing their own proprietary programs to store and secure credit card data.

In June 2005, American Express, Discover Financial Services, JCB, MasterCard Worldwide and Visa International founded the PCI Security Council. These requirements are based on ISO 17799 – the internationally recognized standard for information security practices.

The PCI Security Standards Council is not a policing organization. It does not enforce the PCI DSS, or determine remediation for violations of the PCI DSS.

Enforcement is left to the specific credit card companies and acquirers. Each credit card company separately determines who must be compliant, including any brand-specific enforcement programs. Depending upon the individual credit card company's compliance standards, a system of fines and/or incentives exist to ensure compliance.

PCI DSS applies to every organization that processes credit or debit card information, including merchants and third-party service providers that store, process or transmit credit card/debit card data. Various levels of compliance are established based upon the number of credit card transactions. Under Visa's program, for example, the lowest level of compliance is Level 4, which pertains to companies processing 20,000 to one million annual transactions. These are typically small companies with limited resources to ensure adherence, yet they account for as many as 99% of Visa credit card transactions.

A PCI compliance guide is available at www.pcicomplianceguide.org The PCI Security Standards Council website is www.pcisecuritystandards.org

The Sarbanes-Oxley Act of 2002 (SOX)

The Sarbanes-Oxley Act of 2002, also known as the Public Company Accounting Reform and Investor Protection Act of 2002, sponsored by US Senator Paul Sarbanes and US Representative Michael Oxley, was passed as a result of the large corporate financial scandals involving Enron, WorldCom, Global Crossing and Arthur Andersen. It is commonly referred to simply as SOX. All publicly-traded US companies or non-US companies with a US presence are required to submit an annual report of the effectiveness of their internal accounting controls to the US Securities Exchange Commission. In the U.K. the non-statutory Combined Code of Corporate Governance plays a somewhat similar role to SOX.

SOX contains eleven titles that describe specific mandates and requirements for financial reporting. Provisions of the Sarbanes Oxley Act (SOX) detail criminal and civil penalties for noncompliance, certification of internal auditing, and financial disclosure. SOX is focused on corporate governance and financial disclosure. For the IT manager, the most relevant part of SOX is Section 404: Management Assessment of Internal Controls.

The European Union issued a Directive on Statutory Audit in 2004. Referred to as Europe's SOX, or SOX-lite this directive will, when it is adopted, replace the existing EU 8th Company Law Directive of 1984. SOX-lite clarifies the duties of statutory auditors, provides for their independence and ethical standards, introduces a requirement for external quality assurance, and provides for the public oversight of the audit profession and improved cooperation between oversight bodies in the

European Union. The directive also provides a basis for international co-operation between EU regulators and those in other countries.

The Health Insurance Portability and Accountability Act 1996 (HIPAA)

The Health Insurance Portability and Accountability Act (HIPAA) of 1996 required the US Department of Health and Human Services to adopt national standards for electronic health care transactions. HIPAA mandated the adoption of Federal privacy protections for individually identifiable health information. Effective on April 14, 2001 this rule set national standards for the protection of health information, as applied to the three types of covered entities: health plans, health care clearinghouses, and health care providers who conduct certain health care transactions electronically. Failure to timely implement these standards may, under certain circumstances, trigger the imposition of civil or criminal penalties. To ensure that the privacy rule achieves its intended purpose without adversely affecting the quality of, or creating new barriers to, patient care, in August 2002, the Department adopted modifications necessary to ensure that the privacy rule worked as intended.

HIPAA compliance is not an option – it is a requirement of every entity involved with electronic health care information. Security and privacy are especially important for healthcare organizations using the Internet and web-based applications to exchange what HIPAA refers to as PHI (Protected Health Information).

Organizations required to comply with HIPAA are responsible for among other things: data handling policies and procedures, compliance auditing, and training, limiting physical and network access to approved individuals and auditing all such accesses, data integrity access and modification, non-compliance detection and correction, maintenance of a repository of exact copies of data, as well as continual auditing and certification of compliance. The US Department of Health and Human Services offers a wealth of information regarding HIPAA at: www.hhs.gov/policies/index.html#hippa

Gramm-Leach-Bliley (U.S. Public Law 106-102 – the Financial Services Modernization Act) 1999

Gramm-Leach-Bliley is U.S. Public Law 106-102 – the Financial Services Modernization Act of 1999, which was created to improve consumer financial services by opening up competition between banks, securities and insurance companies. The complex, seven-title law applies to about 9,500 financial institutions. Compliance is mandatory, non-compliance can trigger civil liability and penalties to institutions, and personal liability and penalties to officers and directors.

Security is a crucial part of protecting consumers' personal nonpublic information processed electronically by financial institutions under GLBA. According to the

GLBA's Safeguards Rule financial institutions must ensure security and confidentiality of customer information and protect against threats or hazards to the security or integrity of information, unauthorized access to or use of the customer information.

GLBA requires financial organizations to create a comprehensive, written information security program. GLBA guidelines specify seven steps for development and implementation. Ongoing risk assessment is an integral part of these guidelines.

Compliance is a highly specialized area, which typically requires that you engage an outside firm to conduct a readiness assessment, formulate a holistic compliance plan, and construct reports, perhaps from disparate systems that demonstrate conformance. Much of what is required centers around the general policies and practices of your business. The demand on IT is usually focused on who has access to what information and when. As we discussed above, control of user access can be implemented at the network level using VLAN technology, and at the application level using login credentials. To show compliance, you first need to produce configuration information that identifies your access controls. You also need to demonstrate and report on the successful enforcement of these controls – or any unsuccessful incidents. This is done by logging the users' sessions and reporting on their usage. In order to effectively comply with the auditing provisions in many of these regulations your internal control structures must be automated and continuous. Manual processes don't make sense. The average company trying to implement standards in-house to ensure either regulatory compliance, or simply for their own best practices, has six unique systems for controlling the various areas of security in network. That means six systems to purchase, implement, learn, and maintain... just for security.

There are a number of automated solutions for all areas of compliance. New solutions are constantly evolving to streamline the collection and reporting of compliance information, based on the various regulations that exist. Some managed service providers offer this type of automated solution as a subscription service. This eliminates the need for a major capital outlay, training of your own staff, and on-going maintenance and upgrade of the monitoring system. Look for a provider who will tailor the solution to your environment, your compliance or best practice requirements, and to your security plan.

After you have thoroughly documented your network security plan, it must be communicated to all of your employees. In most organizations, the extent of their security training is giving out passwords and telling users when their passwords need to be changed, either manually or automatically. That is a good start, but you need to actually have security training that outlines your security policy to each employee. In the case of compliance, some regulations specifically call for user training. If you will be putting a security policy in place for the first time, group classes are required. Part of your new employee orientation must also include thorough training on your security policy. It should be more than just a paragraph in your employee handbook. You need to especially emphasize the importance of protecting critical company assets. You need to convey that message with conviction.

You can point to what has happened to companies that have been attacked. For example, you can refer to Amazon's 2004 breach that cost a full 24% drop in their stock the very next day. You can remind them of the TJX credit card fiasco that cost the company an estimated $5 million just to investigate. The pending lawsuits from some 300 banks and countless individuals could cripple the company. In August of 2006 it was reported that hackers got their hands on credit-card account data and personal information for approximately 19,000 customers of an AT&T e-commerce site, and then launched a targeted phishing campaign a few days later that was apparently designed to extract additional information from the affected customers.

Your users have to understand that a single security breach can do irreparable harm to your company. These corporate giants have the resources to recover, but were nonetheless dramatically impacted. Ask yourself and your employees openly and honestly if your company could survive a major security breach. Then tell them how they need to cooperate with you and your IT staff to prevent it.

Remember that lasting change is not achieved through fear, but with exceptional leadership.

Summary

TO keep UGN healthy at level 4, security infrastructure is absolutely essential and must be woven into every aspect of your network. We've summarized some of the critical strategies, written plans, and the key areas of investment below. We have excluded those investments that studies indicate you have already made, so as not to be redundant.

Critical Strategies:

- ◆ Task a holistic approach to security
- ◆ Use a layered approach from the outside and work your way in
- ◆ Use a need-to-know data protection strategy
- ◆ Automate updates, patches, fixes
- ◆ Align security with compliance requirements
- ◆ Monitor continuously
- ◆ Test regularly

Written Plans:

◆ Comprehensive Security Plan

Key Investments:

◆ Network Access Control (NAC)
◆ Firewall with redundancy
◆ VPN solution(s)
◆ Authentication systems
◆ Automated systems for updates, patches, fixes
◆ Regular vulnerability scanning
◆ Compliance consulting, automated testing/reporting as required

Chapter 10

How's UGN Today?

I get a lot of pushback when I suggest that the owner or senior manager of a small to medium sized company should have his/her finger on the pulse of their IT network. The very first question you should ask as you approach any business day is: How is UGN today?

After what you have read so far in this book, I hope you are a convert. If not though, I haven't given up hope. Allow me to take one more crack at it before we're through. Assuming you have a fresh new vision and the belief that you can achieve utility grade performance and effectiveness on your own company's network, and you take the necessary steps to satisfy all of UGN's needs as outlined in the previous chapters, how will you know at any given moment of any business day, if your network is performing at maximum effectiveness? Well there have been major advances in network monitoring and management. Before we get to your role in all of this, we'll take a look at the general case for automated systems that monitor and manage a network.

Somebody has to be watching your network at every moment that your business is running. It is not enough to just see real-time performance. Anything that could be a threat to future performance must also be recognized and reported. In addition, I believe that your network should be monitored hours before your business opens so that you can be sure critical systems are up when your workers show up. The whole idea of your network as a Utility Grade Network (UGN) is that when your employees turn their computers on, it is the same as flipping a light switch: the power necessary to conduct business, in this case in the form of peak performing applications that your employees use to get their jobs done, is instantly there from the moment they press the on button until the moment they shut down for the day.

If you run the type of business that has computer processes going on after hours, or if you have taken advantage of the remote access technologies that extend your employees' work days to anytime day or night, the monitoring must reflect that, and be operational 24/7/365.

The fact is, for many small to medium businesses that is not happening. A 2007 study found that only about ten percent of small to medium businesses use a purchased, non-vendor specific network management system. The other 90 percent use, on average, six different vendor-specific, or shareware (free) network management tools if they do any network management at all. Only about 18 percent of small to medium businesses outsource the management of their network infrastructure, yet of those who do 55 percent of small businesses and 90 percent of medium businesses indicate that they are very satisfied with the service.

Systems management tools exist that can monitor the condition of your network, look for potential problems before they actually affect performance, perform routine configuration and maintenance from a centralized location, keep track of all of your IT assets and their configurations, keep track of and report on compliance related issues as well as security systems and attempts to penetrate those systems, track software versions and the application of vendor supplied upgrades, and eliminate many of the tedious day-to-day tasks that today require countless man-hours of manual labor. Most management systems have some subset of these functions, so that if you were to invest in purchasing all of the necessary systems in-house you would still need to purchase multiple systems, train your IT staff on their use, and invest in on-going support of these systems. Configuring these tools is tedious and time consuming and companies that do invest in monitoring software, often eventually abandon it because of their IT staff's lack of time to maintain it or because they find that the functionality is less than they expected. Their IT staff may even become overwhelmed with the wide range of features that they don't have time to learn. Few small to medium sized companies can afford to hire a full time employee just to configure and maintain the monitoring software.

This accounts, in part, for the research results which indicate that most small to medium sized organizations either decide on nothing or settle for a mixture of several tools that may meet their needs but do not integrate well with each other. Instead what you should do is take inventory of what you need from a holistic viewpoint and choose a partner who can deliver the necessary set of services. The biggest factor in not doing so though is simply that businesses are unaware of what is available. This chapter will focus on what is available.

Let's take a more detailed look at a number of management and support functions that automated systems are able to provide. As you go through this list, try to select the ones that you think make sense for your business. Once you've done that, sit down with your IT folks to determine which of these they are currently performing. Examine how they are performing these functions. Discuss the functions that they are not performing and the value these services would provide for your business. Come up with a comprehensive list of services your business requires based upon these discussions, and then go to your trusted partner to see if they can deliver these services for you. Keep in mind that you may get some resistance from your staff, especially if there are functions they are performing already, perhaps on systems that were purchased. Take a close look at the on-going cost of those systems. Often there are significant annual maintenance costs. In addition, most IT departments in small to medium businesses are understaffed. When companies do look to outsource these monitoring and management functions it is to improve responsiveness. I prefer to use the term right-sourcing because that more accurately describes the approach you need to take. Use a trusted partner where it makes sense, use your own staff where it makes sense, and make sure the two are tightly aligned. That is what I refer to as right-sourcing and it provides the best of both worlds.

We talked a bit about this in Chapter 4. Explain to your limited IT staff that they should be spending more time in Quadrant 2 time-management functions like participating in your technology council and determining what new technologies could potentially drive your business forward, then determining if those technologies are actually mature enough to be effectively deployed. They should also be effectively managing your trusted partner relationship and constantly tweaking their services and contracts to be more effective, and managing the relationships with your connectivity provider(s) for better, faster and less expensive services, higher SLAs, etc. These functions provide significant strategic advantages for your business. There is more than enough daily work to keep them busy, even when you reduce the monotonous and mundane tasks with automation. If it does prove more cost effective to keep some of the existing systems in place, keep them on your radar for replacement once they reach the end of their lifecycle. The availability of qualified services will continue to increase in the marketplace, and the costs as a result, will continue to decrease.

Below are a number of the functions that automated management systems can perform. This is by no means an exhaustive list, and new capabilities are added at an ever increasing rate. If you do right-source some of these functions your IT staff will have more time to keep current on new services as they become available.

Asset Management

Keeping detailed track of the devices on your network can be difficult. An effective stand-alone asset management system or one that is included as a feature in a comprehensive network monitoring and management system or service provides a comprehensive set of asset management features. These features may include:

Asset inventory

A basic list of the devices which includes the manufacturer, make and model number, as well as the serial number of every device. For modular devices, this will also include each of the modules installed in the chassis. For servers and PCs this can include a complete inventory of installed components such as hard drives,

CPU, memory, etc. You may have assets that are connected to your network, which the system will discover automatically, and assets that are not currently connected but that are held as spares in case of an outage, or have reached the end of their lifecycle, but are not completely written off from an accounting perspective. The latter will need to be manually entered if the system is to track them. Additionally, not every system is able to automatically discover every device. The system you choose should be able to identify as many devices as possible on your particular network. For maintenance purposes, manufacturers track support contracts by the serial number of the device under contract. At any time some of your devices may be out to the manufacturer for repair as well.

Software Revisions

As we've stated several times throughout this book, the complex software required to operate networking devices, be they switches, routers, firewalls, file or application servers, etc. is never perfect. Defects in the software are regularly discovered. Sometimes these defects make the device vulnerable to malicious attacks. Other times these defects may affect the device's performance in certain configurations or under certain conditions. This may require that the manufacturer issue a new software revision. The network manager's job includes determining if the new software is necessary for your particular network. If it is, the software revision needs to be applied to any of those particular devices in your network. Depending upon the size of your network, keeping track of the revisions of software on all of the devices on your network manually is just not practical.

Software Licensing

Licensing is a critical issue for every company. A good asset management tool will include the ability to keep track of software licenses and where they are installed. Accurate information regarding which devices have which software installed is a major starting point to effectively managing devices across the network. The system can also ensure that software licenses are appropriately managed so that you are paying for only those copies of particular software that are needed and reduce the risk of fines in a software licensing audit.

History

Not all upgrades work out as planned. It is important to historically track any revision changes to a device, whether hardware or software changes. Sometimes problems occur during the upgrade processes that require you to revert back to the previous revision. Other times a problem only manifests at a later time or in other devices that need to communicate with the device, such that the issue is not immediately obvious. The ability to historically view any revision changes is a valuable tool to resolve these often extremely challenging issues.

Device Monitoring

This is the capability most traditionally associated with network management and includes some or all of these features:

Availability

At the most basic level, a network monitoring system sends out a simple inquiry to each device in your network, referred to as a query. There is a standard that identifies the information that such a query is looking for, and the device's ability to recognize the query and respond properly to it. This is referred to as the Simple Network Management Protocol (SNMP). Without getting into a lot of the technical details behind this standard, suffice to say that every device in your network has to support this standard in order to be monitored effectively. The level to which the device adheres to this standard will determine just how detailed the query can be. There is a more basic query that is available on your PC to test whether a device is powered on and is able to converse using the Internet Protocol that we discussed previously. This is commonly called a ping. If you know the IP address of a device (like the router on your home network for example) and are using a Microsoft Windows operating system, you can click on "start" and then on "run" and type the word ping on the line that comes up, followed by the address of the device you want to test. You will see either a quick response or a message that the ping request has timed out. SNMP performs similar, but much more detailed queries.

Performance

A more sophisticated query can drill down beyond the device's ability to communicate with the monitoring system, and look into how well the device is performing. For example, every device has a central processing unit (CPU) that controls all of the functions of the device. It is helpful to know how much of the CPU's power is being used. A threshold can be set to alert the system administrator when a device's CPU reaches a high level of utilization because at that point the device is likely to be reaching performance affecting overload. By knowing ahead of time, the administrator can either increase the capabilities of the device or make plans to implement a device with higher capability.

This is exactly the type of proactive monitoring you need in your network to keep it performing at peak effectiveness. The system is able to look at every interface on the device (remember our LAN/WAN discussion regarding your home router?) and determine how much information is passing through that interface. This can be compared to the maximum amount of information the interface can handle and again, a threshold setting can alert the administrator when performance may be jeopardized so that proactive measures can be taken. These are just a couple of examples of the many device performance parameters that can be monitored in order to keep all of the critical functions of your network devices functioning properly.

Processes

In addition to the processes inherent to the device itself – the performance of the CPU for example – it is possible to monitor other processes running on a device. This is especially important when monitoring application servers. Think of an e-commerce server for example. I know from a rather painful experience a number of years ago, that is it entirely possible for an e-commerce server to be responding to regular queries, and reporting a well performing and under-utilized CPU, while the critical e-commerce application has stopped running completely. Of course the server itself, regardless of its performance, is only useful if the e-commerce application on the server is actually running! Ensuring that it is, is a necessary capability in your network management system.

Environment

At the basic layer of UGN's hierarchy of needs, the physical environment is critical to each networking device. Network monitoring systems are available that are able to monitor the temperature, humidity, the status of backup battery and UPS systems, to detect smoke or water, and even determine the status of the door(s) to your data center. With IP cameras installed you may even be able to see into the data center from a network management system's display terminals.

Device Management

Management and monitoring are not the same things. Monitoring as the name implies, is a non-intrusive snapshot of the current conditions of a device. The results of monitoring are displayed, stored, compiled and reported as you deem necessary. Management, on the other hand, includes the ability to perform tasks remotely on the devices from a central system. Device Management takes on many forms and performs a variety of tasks. This is where much of the opportunity lies for freeing your staff from mundane, routine processes, but it is certainly not confined to that.

Software Distribution and Provisioning

Installing software from a central location allows new employees to contribute faster, and ensures existing employees can do their job by having the software they need, when they need it. Research has found that centralized management can cut the time it takes to provision new applications in half.

Configuration Management

A critical function for all networks is the creation and maintenance of a configuration management data base (CMDB). Many of today's network management systems include CMDB and store all current and past configurations in this secure database, accessible only by those authorized to see them. A comprehensive versioning system allows for easy restoral of past configurations. Configuration templates are stored and kept available, allowing for network consistency and less risk when deploying new devices.

Fault Isolation

Network management systems, often in combination with a reactive support service, provide root cause analysis for each fault or threshold alarm that occurs, resulting in a proactive solution to a potentially critical issue or the remediation of a current problem or potential future problem. This is the second most widely recognized function of traditional network management systems.

Patch Management

Working in conjunction with the asset management feature of software distribution described above, patch management systems can also distribute the necessary patches and fixes out to the devices on your network. This is extremely helpful in preventing the exploitation of vulnerabilities in your network devices, as previously described. Though similar to the software distribution capability, patch management systems can provide alerts to critical patches that have not been applied which include information on the nature of the patch and purpose of the patch or fix. The administrator can examine this information to determine if it applies to your network in its current configuration. Change for the sake of change on your network should never be allowed, because of the inherent risks during the implementation. It is often a very delicate balancing act. This is a decision that your staff must be capable of and responsible for making. Again, if not bogged down by daily mundane processes, they are better able to stay abreast of current threats and to analyze their potential effect on your network. They should confer with your trusted partner, but maintain responsibility for the ultimate decision to update or not.

Security and Performance Testing and Reporting

Two overarching questions you want to know about UGN include; Is he safe? How well is he performing? There are automated systems that can test critical areas of performance and security and report on the results.

Intrusion Testing

As Nguyen of McAfee points out, you have to try to attack your own network in order to know if it is secure or not. Automated systems can test the security of your network by initiating various types of mock attacks and reporting on the results. In most cases, the companies performing these tests specialize in doing so and are pretty expensive. Compliance mandates may actually require that you have these types of test performed periodically.

Performance Reporting

The latest tools for testing network performance are able to perform a variety of transactions on your critical systems to test the general end-to-end performance of a system or combination of systems, or to test what an end user's experience will be like. The latter are referred to as synthetic transactions and these are being built in to more and more monitoring systems as businesses focus on service delivery as the true measure of IT performance. You can utilize a third party vendor, or perhaps your trusted partner will be able to provide this service. In either case, the system executes a mock transaction and then reports back on how well your network performed. It can be anything from simply accessing a page on your website, to performing a critical accounting function internally.

Access Control

In Chapter 9 we discussed the identity and access management (IAM) approach to access control, and the need to audit and report on who gains access to what systems. This is not typically a function of the network management system, but a more specialized security system. It may be offered as part of a comprehensive network monitoring and maintenance service from a managed service provider (MSP). One of the advantages that an MSP can provide is the ability to obtain a variety of services under one partnership, regardless of the tools or systems necessary to deliver those services. No up-front capital investment, no learning curve, just turn it on and turn it off as you need it.

Displaying and Reporting

How the information that is collected by the network management system is reported varies considerably between the many products and services available. Most systems offer network maps, dashboards, charts, graphs, lists, and countless combinations of these. The vast majority of them are designed to be viewed by thoroughly trained and knowledgeable IT staff. There are various levels of views that typically start out as broad views that provide up or down status and allow the user to drill down deeper into a particular network segment, and then perhaps into a particular device, and then into modules within that device or interfaces on the device. All along the way the information that is provided gets more and more cryptic and detailed. For a seasoned IT professional these are great tools with tremendous power. With enough knowledge the IT guru can have every bit of information about your network, everything connected to it, every configuration, etc. Without the right knowledge, however, the information is just plain overwhelming. It is no wonder that many small to medium sized businesses abandon these high powered solutions and revert back to manually viewing the network via the various configuration interfaces that they are already familiar with.

It often happens that these complex systems are utilized for little more than a network map to alert the IT staff when a fault has occurred, at which time they use the configuration interface to go into the device and start looking for the root cause of the problem. The challenge with this approach is that your network continues to get more and more complex, and the systems and devices rely on each other, so that finding the root cause device by device can waste precious recovery time. We will talk about support mechanisms and what has to happen when a fault condition occurs in a little while.

I want to specifically address the need for you to be in the loop here. As you pay more attention to IT as a strategy for driving your business as opposed to a necessary expense, I believe you must have your finger on the pulse of your IT network. The problem is that this is an approach that is only starting to get the attention of the developers of network monitoring and management systems.

There has been a trend over the last few years to move from network maps to performance dashboards in how the information is displayed. The rationale is that a dashboard provides key performance indicators, much like the dashboard of a vehicle. Most of these dashboards still provide analytical statistics for a variety of very technical functions that network devices perform continuously. The average non-technical person has absolutely no idea what these things are or what they mean. A few companies have begun to design and implement executive dashboards that are able to report on how well services are being delivered. Those synthetic transactions discussed earlier can tell you how long it takes for a user to do something. If you are using an IP based phone system, the call management software can tell your network management system how long customers are waiting to speak to someone. That type of information is useful to your company and to those in charge of the various related functions.

I have a suggestion for what the ideal dashboard should tell you as the business owner or senior manager. I haven't been able to find anything that fits it, but I have had this discussion with a few vendors, most of whom say it is possible but not on their product roadmap. If enough people buy this book and make enough noise, perhaps one day we'll see this dashboard available. So here is what I think it should show you:

1. A high level map of all of your infrastructure equipment locations, each of which appears shaded in either green (everything is fine) red (something is down hard) or yellow (there is a potential problem brewing).

2. The ability to click on any one of these locations and see the environmental conditions we described earlier, and every infrastructure device or server; each of them color shaded as described above. A red condition could be caused by a module in the device, or a process that has stopped running on a server. You don't need to go to the module level in your display.

3. The ability to click on each red device and see exactly how many users are affected by the red condition of that device/server – be it a single module/ service or the entire device/server that is down, and who those users are by category. Possible categories would be internal staff by functional group, customers, and suppliers.

4. Clicking on that device/server should also show you how much productivity or revenue per hour is affected by the effected device/module or server/ service. It should be a simple calculation like we had in Chapter 1: weighted average cost per employee per hour x number affected, average revenue per employee/customer per hour x number affected.

5. The ability to click on each yellow device/server and see how the device is performing against its peak performance along with the same information as the red alarm.

6. A real time report on any problems that have occurred this month and how long it took to resolve them, along with how much the problem cost your business. In addition, you should be able to print these reports each month.

That is really all I want for your business owner's dashboard. That would be my ultimate definition of having your finger on the pulse of your IT. You might want it to be a little different. My point is that there needs to be an IT dashboard to tell you if you are bleeding money. Thus the real need for a red alarm. All the rest of the information that systems currently provide can be presented to IT folks or to mid-level managers, who do what they have to do with it.

Since this dashboard is not available – yet – and I still believe you need your finger on the pulse, the only practical way for that to happen is for you to insist on getting this information manually. Management software does produce alerts. An alert not only results in the change of displayed information, but also sends out the information related to the change in condition to whatever devices it has the capability to send to. An alert can result in an e-mail, a phone call, a text message, a page, pretty much any way that communication can take place. In addition, someone has to react to the alert and take corrective action. Most network management systems also have the ability to automatically notify a call ticketing system which results in a call ticket that prompts the necessary corrective action. Call ticketing systems often have automatic escalation processes that run, and generate their own alerts when the ticket has not been addressed or resolved in a timely manner. My suggestion is that you insert yourself into the notification process with a clearly defined set of criteria for when you want to be informed of an outage, potential outage, or security breach. This is not a case of what you don't know won't hurt you. We have already established that what you don't know is costing you dearly.

So I stretched the truth a little at the end there, since I started that whole list by saying these were some of the many functions that management systems perform today. Regardless, there are some great management systems and services in use and readily available. As we discussed at the start of this chapter, the best way to put them into practice after you and your IT staff have determined what your needs are, is to engage your trusted partner. If you've engaged the right partner as outlined in Chapter 5 you will end up with a custom tailored, cost effective solution that results in a cooperative effort between your partner and your staff to assure your network is protected, compliant, and performing effectively. And you will not have to ask – you will know exactly how UGN is doing.

Chapter 11
Final Thoughts on UGN and His Future

Recap

IT is broken, and it is up to you, business owners and senior managers, to fix it. Small to medium sized businesses are bleeding money in lost productivity as the statistics we've presented firmly demonstrate. IT people cannot fix the problem by themselves or they would have done so. The products and tools available in the market are collectively able, when properly combined and supported, to stop the bleeding. The problem is leadership.

Stopping the bleeding is no small task. There are no such things as quick and easy fixes, as with most problems we face in this world. Change is possible, and it takes three things:

◆ Leadership
◆ A paradigm shift
◆ Hope that real change is possible

You have to provide all three of these for your company's IT investments to truly drive your company forward.

This is a very exciting time for Information Technology. The rate of advancement in technology is at its greatest point in the history of the world. All indications are that it will continue to accelerate.

At the same time, the IT talent pool continues to shrink. Making the most effective use of those resources is going to be the key to your ability to bring about real lasting change.

You must take a vested interest in leading the change. From a company with an average network, bleeding 3.6 percent of gross revenues in lost productivity due to poor network performance you can become a company with a robust, effective network that delivers technology as a service that drives business.

You must make it clear that technology is not viewed as a necessary evil moneypit, but is a strategic tool for maximum performance and productivity at all levels of your organization.

You must create a vision for a true Utility Grade Network that is not only achievable but sustainable, and will not only pay for itself in productivity gains, but will lead to increased revenue and decreased costs.

The first thing you have to do is evaluate your IT staff. If the people on your staff do not fit the criteria outlined in Chapter 4, you need to make adjustments to your roster, and you need to do it quickly. If they do meet the criteria, they will welcome your newfound interest in their ultimate success. And they will support you every step.

The second thing you have to do is determine where your staff is strong and where they are not. In the areas where they are not strong you will need to find a trusted partner to augment your staff. Engage in dialogue with potential partners before you specifically need them for a project or service. These should be philosophical discussions to find a fit between your companies and staffs.

Then you must set the plan into motion for achieving your UGN vision.

Your action plan must include a number of topics that we've covered in this book:

1. Form a Technology Council.
2. Engage your Trusted Partner.
3. Introduce UGN.
4. Address UGN's hierarchy of needs from the bottom up by:
    a. Assessing the current status of each layer.
    b. Identifying deficiencies in each layer.
    c. Formulating a plan to address those deficiencies.
5. Invest in a proactive monitoring service.
6. Include yourself in the escalation notification process.
7. Invest in reactive support.
8. Adopt the technology lifecycle model.

After you have attained Utility Grade status and are sure UGN is healthy, and sustainably so, and that your IT network is effective, you are able to move on to the much touted issue of alignment.

Alignment is best achieved by viewing IT as a service, where the applications and support provided by the IT function in your business is considered to be a set of essential services. This is a step up from what we have advocated in the Utility Grade Network paradigm.

Remember this stark truth so you don't get ahead of yourself: companies that try to achieve alignment on an ineffective IT network can end up worse than when they started. It is like building your house on sand instead of solid ground. Don't do it. Forget what the so-called experts are telling you. The facts speak loudly enough by themselves to warrant your complete attention.

UGN's future

There are some emerging technologies and solutions that will likely become a part of your strategy or become issues you need to deal with. In fact you may already have some of these incorporated in or affecting your network.

We'll cover a few of the trends that are gaining traction and showing promise:

The Information Technology Infrastructure Library (ITIL®)

The Information Technology Infrastructure Library (ITIL®) that we discussed in Chapter 7 has enjoyed widespread popularity among larger enterprise IT organizations. With the recent release of version 3, which is being touted as appropriate for smaller organizations, we are going to be hearing a lot more about it. Everyone is going to include ITIL® language into their marketing.

ITIL® consulting firms for the SMB market are going to be coming out of the woodwork. Solution providers will also start tailoring their approaches and their solutions to the ITIL® model.

All of this will be occurring as you embark on your action plan. It may be worthwhile having a look at ITIL® and attending an ITIL® class or seminar to see if it can be worked into your plan. We have not typically engaged very large firms in our business, but I know they are pursuing the service delivery model it touts. I would welcome your feedback when and if you look into it.

Software as a Service (SaaS)

Software as a Service (SaaS) is available today from a number of service providers. It offers the ability to subscribe to the use of a software application on a per user basis. There are typically none of the up-front fees associated with launching a new application such as buying the software and licenses along with the server(s) and storage associated with the application. Perhaps the most well known to date is Salesforce.com. We use their services ourselves and are impressed. A lot is being said about SaaS, some of it accurate, some of it not. This much is true: for certain applications SaaS is a good fit for many organizations. You most likely cannot convert to a wholesale SaaS model since it unlikely that all of your applications can be replaced with a SaaS offering immediately, and SaaS does not negate the need for an IT infrastructure in your company. You still need a network infrastructure on which to connect your PCs and to run your in-house applications.

SaaS is sometimes confused with the old Application Service Provider (ASP) model that allowed standard applications to be run at an offsite location. It amounted to taking out the server and storage portion of UGN's Server/PC and Peripheral Infrastructure layer and placing it off-site. It didn't work out too well because the ASPs themselves had trouble getting end users to trust that their data would be secure. Because of the lack of traction in the market, and the burst of the dot.com bubble, many ASPs went out of business. Others did quite well. The major difference in the SaaS model is that the applications have been developed as web applications instead of traditional applications with a web enabling front end. SaaS is only going to get better and more widely adopted as time goes on.

Appliance-based Software Delivery (AbSD)

Appliance-based Software Delivery (AbSD) has crept onto the scene over the last decade and includes many of the qualities found in SaaS:

◆ Easy installation and configuration

◆ Web-based interface

◆ Automatic application data feeds, maintenance, and upgrades

◆ Automatic data recovery and backup

AbSD also offers several characteristics not found in SaaS:

◆ A dedicated, high performance hardware platform

◆ A secure, on-premise deployment

◆ A traditional upfront purchase, subscription license, or a combination of the two.

Some AbSD solutions directly compete with SaaS. An appliance called SugarCube offers Salesforce.com-like functionality in a box touted as a reliable, secure, on-premise solution at a cost that is comparable to, or less than, the SaaS offering we mentioned above. Sometimes SaaS doesn't make sense because of security considerations or architectural reasons and AbSD can be an attractive alternative to customers. AbSD is becoming particularly popular among IT support staff with products that offer automation of routine tasks such as software distribution, change management, NAC management, IAM management, etc. Once again a note of caution; these are what we referred to as point products in Chapter 7. If your primary vendor offers a similar product in their portfolio that has a common look and feel, as well as a common monitoring, management and support interface, take a hard look at it, and make an informed decision.

Cisco Certified Design Expert (CCDE)

The Cisco Certified Design Expert (CCDE) is a new certification just announced in January 2008. Cisco Systems has the most widely recognized vendor specific certification program in the IT industry. The highest level of their existing certification program is the coveted Cisco Certified Internetworking Expert (CCIE). An IT professional having attained CCIE status is widely recognized as an expert across multiple IT disciplines and commands a great deal of respect. The new program promises to be just as rigorous and those achieving CCDE status will be recognized as experts in the design of network infrastructures such as we discussed in Chapter 7, Backbone Network Infrastructure. Cisco require that their highest level direct partners have CCIE certified technicians on staff. Talk to your trusted partner about their plans to incorporate this new certification into their staff.

Blogs, wikis, forums, and other on-line networking community tools

These on-line networking community tools are not new. Their use is increasing steadily among corporate employees. The Yankee Group (YG) says the IT department's control of applications and services is slipping because of "consumerization" – the adoption of consumer technologies in the corporate environment. According to *Zen and the Art of Rogue Employee Management*, a recently released YG report, nearly 50 percent of employees feel more empowered than the IT department of their company to control their own personal IT environment. The report says IT departments that fail to recognize the adoption of these technologies in the workplace could end up with a hazardous mix of secured and unsecured applications on the corporate network.

It's time for a new operating model; an IT care co-op is the solution. The report recommended some best practices for a Zen-like approach to an IT care co-op solution:

- ◆ Using Web 2.0 tools to create customer care cooperatives that save IT time and money while improving end-user satisfaction.
- ◆ Facilitating online social networks and wikis, which allow end-user communities to manage their own IT support functions.
- ◆ Setting security baselines that aren't flexible for IT groups to gracefully stitch wikis and collaborative tools into your protected network.

In case you are tempted to ban the use of these on-line communities entirely, you should note that a 2007 survey of IT professionals showed that 93 percent of them said that they participate in on-line communities, and that they are significantly more productive as a result. This is largely due to their ability to research, and ask questions of and share experiences with peers.

Federation

Federation refers to an innovative technology that enables access from external domains, similar to how you allow your existing users to access various applications within your company's network. Federation is on the radar of most large enterprise organizations. By its very nature federation requires tight policies and controls. Products are emerging to automate the setup and control of federations. It is only a matter of time until widespread adoption requires your company to look at it.

Role Tailored Business Productivity Software

This is a phrase used by Microsoft to describe their approach to a new software product called Microsoft Dynamics™. It sort of takes the Service Oriented Architecture (SoA) approach that large enterprises have been focused on for delivering IT as a ubiquitous service, and applies it to a Microsoft-centric platform. The idea is that you can empower your employees by tailoring their desktop to exactly how they work each day. You can put the information they need to get their job done right at their fingertips. They don't need to know what specific application holds the data and go searching for a particular spreadsheet or report or document from a particular location. Instead the data is presented automatically, while the search and retrieval happens behind the scenes automatically. I found the white paper to be fascinating. You can see for yourself by visiting: http://www.microsoft.com/dynamics

Web 2.0

Though the name Web 2.0 seems to imply a "new Internet" that is not the case. Web 2.0 simply refers to the transition on the Internet from a tool used primarily to acquire information and to conduct one-way business transactions such as e-commerce, to more of a large community of users where human interactions result in content that is published, managed, and used by the community in a more socially oriented way. This term was made popular during a conference in 2004 and has been widely adopted since.

Technology continues to thrive at a rapid pace. Your UGN will be ready...

142

Appendix A
Assessing the Test

The test is designed as a simple tool to guide you through the remainder of this book. Every network is different and so is the condition of every network I have ever encountered. Mastery in one area seldom means mastery in all. The Test is intended to establish a priority list for the reading of chapters in this book. I've identified the chapter(s) associated with each of the questions below.

Where you answered

a)   you're in good shape and can either skip or glance over the chapter(s) later.

b)   you should review the associated chapter(s) at your leisure to see if you can improve that area.

c)   you should make it a priority to read the associated chapter(s) first in the order in which those questions appear.

d)   As soon as you finish reading these chapters, turn your attention to those chapters associated with every question to which you've answered d). What you don't know could be hurting you, but it might not be. Make a list of those and get some answers so that you can re-test those questions and give them the attention they need.

Answer Key

Here, then, are the associated chapters:

1)   Which best describes your IT staff: **Chapter 4**

2)   Which best describes your company's relationship with IT suppliers: **Chapter 5**

3)   Which best describes your computer room: **Chapter 6**

4)   Which best describes your IT equipment purchasing strategy: **Chapters 5 & 7**

5)   Which best describes the documentation available on your IT network: Chapter 7

6)   Which best describes your e-mail and Internet connections: **Chapters 7 & 8**

7)   Which best describes the performance of your major applications: **Chapter 7 & 8**

8)   How are you informed of critical outages or attacks on your network? **Chapter 10**

9)   Which best describes your backup and disaster recovery plan: **Chapter 8**

10) Which best describes your IT security policy: **Chapter 8**

11) Which best defines your overall opinion regarding IT: **Chapter 11**

When you've completed all of the chapters you needed to read, be sure to read the short summary and glimpse into the future in Chapter 11. It gives you the bottom line on the approach required to assure your network is as good as it can be, based on your willingness to invest in the level of effectiveness your business needs. Every aspect of how your business operates is determined by your attitude toward, and leadership of, IT. That is truly the bottom line.

Appendix B
Glossary of Terms

AbSD (Appliance-based Software Delivery): An offering similar to SaaS, except that the software is installed on a dedicated appliance that is located on the customer's premises, and the appliance and software can either be purchased outright, billed on a per user basis, or offered as a combination of the two.

Alignment: In technology terms alignment refers to the process of strategically investing in software applications and technology services that directly support business operations.

ASP (Application Service Provider): Outsourced service providers that allowed standard applications to be run on servers at an offsite location and accessed by a company's users via the Internet or a dedicated circuit from the users' site(s) to the ASP's location. Largely migrated to or replaced by SaaS providers.

BICSI: A professional association supporting the information transport systems (ITS) industry with information, education and knowledge assessment for individuals and companies.

Blog: A website used to provide commentary or news on a particular subject. A blog allows text, images, and links to other blogs, web pages, etc. Users typically are able to leave comments in an interactive format which is reviewed by an administrator.

CMDB (Configuration Management Database): A software solution for storing the configurations of devices on a network, for archiving various revisions to those configurations, and ensuring that the most current configurations are instantly accessible to those responsible for maintaining the network.

Combined Code of Corporate Governance: The non-statutory compliance code in the U.K. that plays a somewhat similar role to SOX.

Convergence: In technology terms convergence generally refers to the merging of voice, data, and video applications on a single, digital network infrastructure. Some have recently used the term to describe a process of developing a new product or service strategy utilizing technology, and weaving the use of technology into the plan.

CPU (Central Processing Unit): The main integrated circuits chip in a computing device which controls the execution of software routines run on that device.

Dashboard: A high level display of information regarding the performance of a network, provided by a network monitoring/management system.

Demarc (Demarcation point): Typically refers to the point where you are allowed to connect to a circuit provided by your carrier or Internet service provider.

DHCP (Dynamic Host Configuration Protocol): A software program that accepts requests for IP addresses from clients, and provides a valid address along with other information the client will need to effectively communicate on the network.

DMZ (DeMilitarized Zone): A network segment that exists between the Internet and a corporate network which is separated by a firewall to assure that outside users can gain access to servers on the DMZ, while being prevented from accessing any resources on the corporate network.

DNS (Domain Name Service): A software service that provides the IP address of a service, such as a website or e-mail service, when a client machine requests the location of the service whose URL has been entered into a web browser running on the client machine. This is the most common understanding, though it is not entirely technically accurate. A more detailed technical description is beyond the scope of this book.

Downtime: The time when technology is not functioning properly and users are either not able to access or use the technology, or the technology is performing too poorly in order for users to effectively perform their jobs.

EBITDA: Refers to a company's Earnings Before Interest, Taxes, Depreciation, and Adjustments better known as the bottom line.

Firewall: A security device that controls the flow of information between an outside network, such as the Internet, and a company's internal network. A firewall can perform a variety of security, and general network functions such as NAT and DHCP.

Five Nines: A term used to describe the reliability of a network which represents 99.999 percent uptime.

GLBA (The Gramm-Leach-Bliley Act of the US): Includes a Safeguards Rule which requires that financial institutions ensure the security and confidentiality of customer information and protect against threats or hazards to the security or integrity of information as well as unauthorized access to or use of the customer information.

Hacker: Anyone who accesses a computer network without specific permission to do so. Typically refers to an individual who does so with malicious intent.

Hijacking: The process of taking over a legitimate harmless session for the purpose of gaining unauthorized access to systems or resources on a network.

HIPAA (Health Insurance Portability and Accountability Act): Effective on April 14, 2001 this law mandated the adoption of Federal privacy protections for individually identifiable health information and set national standards for the protection of health information, required of every entity involved with health care information.

Host: Any computing device connected to a network and assigned an IP address.

HVAC (Heating Ventilation and Air Conditioning): Used for climate control in the computer room or data center for the purposes of this book.

IAM (Identity and Access Management): The security measures that an organization employs to control who gets access to what. It can range from a simple system of passwords to a complex system of security badges, tokens, and even biometric security devices.

IM (Instant Messaging): A software service that allows users to open "chat" sessions with other users for instantaneous text messaging across a private network, the Internet, or both.

Infrastructure: A general term used to describe a combination of equipment, software, and services that are interconnected to perform a set of critical functions required to support higher level functions on a network.

IP (Internet Protocol): The software language that networking devices use to connect to, and identify themselves on, a network.

IPAM (Internet Protocol Address Management): The process of managing the procurement, distribution, control, and documentation of IP addresses for an organization.

IPT (Internet Protocol Telephony): The use of the Internet Protocol as a method of allowing telephone systems and devices, which normally operate on a separate network, to operate on a digital data network.

ISP (Internet Service Provider): Self explanatory.

ITIL® (Information Technology Infrastructure Library): A set of best practice standards for Information Technology developed by the UK's Office of Government Commerce.

LAN (Local Area Network): A network of computers, peripherals, and networking devices confined to a relatively small area – usually not beyond a single building.

Life-Cycle: In technology this refers to the time from implementation of a product or technology solution until the product or solution is no longer able to adequately support the needs of your business.

Malware: Malicious software that is intended to harm or disrupt the performance of a network and/or particular devices on the network.

Maslow's Hierarchy: A layered approach to explaining human needs as developed by Dr. Abraham Maslow.

MDA (Main Distribution Area): TIA term referring to the wiring you put in place from the demarc to your internal backbone infrastructure.

MSP (Managed Service Provider): A company that provides outsourced network monitoring and management services.

MTTR (Mean Time to Repair): The time it takes from detection of a problem in a device or system to the restoral of full functionality to that device or system.

NAC (Network Access Control): For the purpose of this book the process, methods and systems controlling who can gain access to your network.

NAS (Network Attached Storage): Standalone dedicated file servers or disk arrays used to store data on a network.

NAT (Network Address Translation): The process of changing an internal, private address for an external public address on IP networks, and vice versa.

NCPI (Network Critical Physical Infrastructure): The facilities, equipment, and services that comprise the computer room or data center, and any additional distributed location that house networking equipment and provide for power, climate, and security necessary to assure maximum operating conditions for that equipment.

Network Integrator: Another name for a VAR.

PCI DSS (Payment Card Industry Data Security Standard): Standards established and enforced by individual credit card companies to ensure secure handling of credit card transactions by merchants accepting payment using the respective credit cards.

Peer-to-Peer Network: A network of computers that are connected to each other and are set up to share information and resources with each other without a central server.

PIN (Personal Identification Number): Most often associated with an ATM card, this refers to any number uniquely identified with a particular user which is used to gain access to a network or device.

PING (Packet Inter-Network Groper): A software routine that sends an echo request to a device on a network, and waits for an echo response. The response indicates that the device is able to respond, and the time and the path it takes for the response to arrive can be indicative of the performance of the network, and of other devices along the path.

Protocol: A software programming language used to control the flow of information inside of and between computers, peripherals and/or networking devices.

Rootkit: A set of tools often loaded onto a server or PC that has been breached by a hacker, intended to conceal running processes, files or system data from the operating system of the violated system. The concealed processes can then be used to damage the system or to infect or retrieve information from unsuspecting users who access the violated system.

SaaS (Software as a Service): An outsourced service that offers the ability to subscribe to the use of software applications on a per user basis, i.e. SalesForce.com

SAN (Storage Area Network): A pool of storage using interconnected storage devices and a common communication and control channel used to store large amounts of data on a network.

Security Infrastructure: The total collection of hardware and software systems embedded in a network to protect it from unauthorized access, loss or theft of data, or malicious damage.

Server: A computer specifically designed to run software applications for a network of users.

Session: Refers to a period of time when a user on a computer has gained access to a service on a server. A common example is when a consumer accesses a website.

SNMP (Simple Network Management Protocol): A standardized protocol language used in network monitoring systems that defines how a device communicates with the system in order to report on the condition of various systems or functions within the device.

SOX (The Sarbanes-Oxley Act of 2002): Also known as the Public Company Accounting Reform and Investor Protection Act of 2002, sponsored by US Senator Paul Sarbanes and US Representative Michael Oxley. It requires all publicly-traded US companies or non-US companies with a US presence to submit an annual report of the effectiveness of their internal accounting controls to the US Securities Exchange Commission.

SOX-lite: Also known as Europe's SOX. A Directive on Statutory Audit issued by the European Union in 2004 which will, when it is adopted, replace the existing EU 8th Company Law Directive of 1984.

Spoofing: The process of disguising a potentially harmful session as if it were a legitimate harmless session, often used by hackers.

TCO (Total Cost of Ownership): Refers to the combined costs of acquisition and support of a product for its entire lifecycle.

TCP (Transport Control Protocol): The software language that runs on top of the IP protocol that networking devices use to communicate with each other.

Telecom: Short for telecommunications and usually used to describe the network circuits and equipment that carry voice communication.

TIA -942: The TIA's Telecommunications Infrastructure Standard for Data Centers which specifies the minimum requirements for both telecommunications and facilities infrastructures, and establishes a topology for connecting and accessing these elements.

TIA (The Telecommunications Industry Association): An industry trade association that publishes voluntary standards widely recognized and implemented in the information technology industry.

UGN: Eugene, a fictitious character who represents your utility grade network.

UGN (Utility Grade Network): A network that is available and performing at maximum potential during critical operating hours.

UGN's Hierarchy: A layered approach to explaining what is needed in order to obtain and maintain utility grade performance of your network as developed by the author.

UPS (Uninterruptible Power Supply): A device that is placed between a power source and a powered device for the purpose of protecting the device from fluctuations in the source that might be damaging, and of providing power to the device for a pre-determined period should source power be lost or interrupted.

Uptime Institute: An industry provider of vendor-neutral, research-based information on high-density enterprise computing recognized as a trusted source of information to industry users, vendors, and the media.

Uptime: The time when technology is functioning properly and users are able to access and use the technology to effectively perform their jobs.

URL (Universal Resource Locator): The common name for a string of characters that represent a resource on a network. It is most commonly identified with the string of characters entered into a web browser when a client seeks to find a website on the Internet.

VAR (Value Added Reseller): A term used to describe a company that sells technology products or solutions and adds additional value to the customer either in designing, implementation, or support of the technology they sell.

VLAN (Virtual Local Area Network) Software configuration through networking devices that allow multiple hosts to logically appear as connected to the same network even thought the devices are physically connected to different networks. This is usually done for security reasons.

VPN (Virtual Private Network): A secure connection between two hosts that encrypts data between the hosts for security of the data as it travels across the network. Usually used for connections going across the Internet.

WAN (Wide Area Network): Network devices and physical circuits that are used to connect local area networks to other local area networks. They are typically provided by telephone companies or Internet Service Providers, or a combination of these.

YouTube: A free social networking Internet site that allows users to view and post video clips and to join groups with similar interests. Log in is required to access certain types of videos.

Index

INService 55

A

AbSD (Appliance-based Software Delivery) 140
Alignment 2, 76, 139
American Society of Heating, Refrigerating and Air-Conditioning Engineers (ASHRAE) 67

B

Backbone Network Infrastructure 11, 75-90
  change management 85
  configuration archiving 84
  documentation 87
  level of redundancy 82
  maintenance 86
  monitoring 86
  network design 80
  security 83
  spare parts 84
  vendor, equipment 80, 94
BICSI 72
Business Continuity Planning 92

C

Cabling 71
Certifications 57
Change Management 31, 85
Change or Die 5
Chief Information Officer (CIO) 41
Cisco Certified Design Expert (CCDE) 141
Clean Agent Fire Suppression Systems 70

Combined Code of Corporate Governance 119
compliance 118
Configuration Archiving 84
Configuration Management 131
  configuration management data base (CMDB) 84, 131
Convergence 3

D

demarcation (demarc) point 71
Device Management 130
Device Monitoring 129
Digital certificates 116
Directive on Statutory Audit 119
DMZ (DeMilitarized Zone) 97
domain 101
  DNS (domain name service) 78
Downtime
  cost 10
  costs of enterprise 8
Dynamic Host Configuration Protocol (DHCP) 77

E

e-mail 102
  e-mail system 13
Earnings Before Interest, Taxes, Depreciation, and Amortization (EBITDA) 9

F

Federation 142